Me & My DJ

My Life as the wife of DJ K-Rock, Mrs. Kennith Michael Moorer

by Rayna Bias-Moorer
2013

Prologue

I do not like that photo of Kennith and I on our wedding day. I could have, and should have looked so much better. The weeks leading up to that day wrought havoc in my life. And as I look at this photo, I see the confusion, the pain, the hurt, the longing, and the brokenness I felt. I felt exactly how I looked in that picture, a mess.

I need healing. My children need healing.

That is why I am writing this book, nothing more and nothing less.

I believe that the truth will set me free, and this is my truth.

When I told my children, I was writing a book about my marriage, my kids laughed...and then they encouraged me. The biggest lesson I want them to learn is we cannot change yesterday, but we can change every tomorrow.

My children have taught me resilience. I pray I have taught them to always keep it real, treat people the way you want to be treated, and that the acceptance of truth, no matter how ugly, is always the best way to face tomorrow.

Forgiveness has been the key to my survival. I am struggling very hard to be able to forgive all. Hopefully, when the last word is written, I will have accomplished this goal.

It is not my goal to hurt or embarrass anyone. I am simply revealing my own truths in the hope that I can be healed of pain, fear, and bitterness.

In the hope that I can love again.

DEDICATION

For My Momma, the strongest woman I know. Had it not been for your prayers, where would we be?

For My Kali & My Malachi...You are the sparkles in my eyes, my Gifts from God. You are Love immeasurable. I became "Me" the day I became your Gammies!

For My Four Babies...Marcel, Shayna, KJ, and Myles...Never, ever, never, not for one moment, have I ever regretted YOU. Each of you were made in love, and I would tolerate every single moment of pain again and again and again if it meant I would be your Mom!

For My God-Daughters...Brianna and Haile. You, too, have paid the price for a failed marriage. I wish I could have been a part of all your firsts. I Love You, and You will always have your special place in my heart.

For K...Kennith, Thank You for My Kids.

Me & My DJ

Loyal to a Fault

I am the baby of my family. My Mexican Mother and my Black Father made four adorable little mixed girls. And since my Father, Gerald Lee Bias, didn't have any sons, and I was the last child to be born to the family, I was named Rayna Geraldine Bias. My Mother, Yvonne (Vargas) Bias, tells the story of how she was so upset that she cussed my Father out and threatened to have an abortion when she found out that she was pregnant with me. It doesn't hurt my feelings; I know she is glad to have me.

I was born January 18th, 1970. And the IUD my Mom had in to prevent an unwanted pregnancy came out right after me. Regardless of what I have been told, I have always felt loved and never once felt unwanted. When God has something for you, there is nothing anyone can do to change it. I was meant to be.

My family was not rich, and we weren't poor. Well, sometimes I guess we were very close to poor, but, we survived. I thought we were middle class. My parents owned a home, and we always had at least one car, and sometimes two. There were times when money was thin, but, truthfully my older sisters experienced more of those tough times than I did.

My earliest memory as a child was lying on a blanket on the grass in the front yard with my Mother and staring up at the stars. I can't recall ever missing my Mother when I was young. She was ever present. I used to lie with her on the couch, me resting my head in the bend of her knees as she laid on her side reading or watching TV. I thought my Mother was beautiful, and I knew she was good.

My Mother and I posing in our den on Waters Street in Pomona. 1972

When I was three, my Daddy had open-heart surgery. He had suffered a Heart Attack and my family rushed around, back and forth to Hollywood where he was hospitalized, and I was often left with babysitters. Although no one really ever sat with me and tried to explain what was going on with my Daddy, I knew a lot wasn't right. I listened intently to talks and whispers and my imagination ran wild. I had learned early to be quiet and good when there was tension in the house. So, I quieted myself and listened and watched for clues as to why my Daddy was gone. When the day came that I could finally go and see him, I waited in the big waiting room with all the big glass windows. I looked up at the people who passed, some looked sick and some looked worried. I wondered how my Daddy would look.

When I saw him sitting in the wheelchair, he looked frail. I had never seen him look frail before, and his eyes were dark. He had tubes and things coming out of him, and I quietly sat and waited to know when I could touch him. I was excited to see my Daddy, but, I didn't show it. My Dad didn't hug or touch us a lot, so, I am not sure why I expected his touch, but on that day, I craved it. He finally looked over at me and called me to him. I stood there shyly and he put his arms out for me to come closer. Somebody helped me to climb up and sit on his lap. I immediately felt better.

My Father couldn't work anymore, so he became my primary caregiver. He would be there when I woke up in the morning, and he would guide me as I washed up and dressed for the day. If he didn't take me to the local coffee shop for breakfast, he would fix me breakfast at home. I would go everywhere he went, to the store, to pay bills, to see his friends, to doctor's appointments, and to people's houses where he would do odd jobs for people or just sit around talking and drinking beer. I liked being with my Daddy, when it was just us.

Me, on my
Daddy's Lap.
1973

My older sisters loved me. At least two of them did.

Wanda was my oldest sister, and ten years my senior. She was

always about business, always trying to do what's right, a typical

firstborn child. She's adventurous and protective. I have always

felt like she didn't just love me, but, that she liked me. The

second born, Karla, was right behind Wanda and nine years

older than I. Karla was distant at times, more of an introvert and

never a push over. Both of my older sisters would handle things,

I always felt safe in their care. My third sister, Patricia, is six

years older than I am. There were times when she liked me and

times when she didn't. Most days she didn't. She was always

consumed with herself, and I was just a tag-a- long and a bother. My earliest memory of her was putting a big wad of toilet paper in my butt cheeks, when she was supposed to be helping me to wipe my behind after using the toilet. I would yell "COME and WIPE ME!" and one of the three would have to stop whatever they were doing to come and ensure that my behind was cleaned properly. If one of my sisters were playing outside or visiting the neighbors, I would yell out "CROSS ME CROSS THE STREET!" and if I yelled it loud and long enough either one of them or a neighbor would feel sorry for me and come and help me across the street. I was a brat, but, it was either that or I would have to spend time at home alone. I still spent most of my time at home. I read through the entire Encyclopedia Set my parents bought from the traveling salesman. I was reading by the age of three, and actually comprehending. Reading was my escape from boredom, it was a big deal and the fact that I could read at such a young age brought me a lot of attention. I enjoyed when my parents and my sisters would brag about my reading ability.

My sister, Trish, got a kick out of telling me that I was adopted and giving me all the supporting evidence to prove that I was not her real sister. She was very convincing. She pointed out that my hair was longer, I was the only one that wore glasses, and I didn't look black like my Daddy. I almost believed her. I was so anxious about it that one day I sobbed to my Mom, and my Mom told me that I was all hers. That was all it took, I believed my Momma. Besides I had heard the stories about almost being aborted. If my Mom didn't want her own baby, she definitely wouldn't take someone else's.

My sisters and I,
1972.
Wanda, Karla,
Patricia and
Rayna Bias.

My two older sisters spent a lot of time with me, they

would take me places. I went to all the High School Games, and

they took even me with them on dates, sometimes. I loved the

attention I would get from their friends and schoolmates.

Everyone would tell me how cute I was, especially

complimenting me on my thick, long, wavy, black hair. Both of

my oldest sisters didn't date different dudes, they pretty much

had the same boyfriends through High School and later. Their boyfriends were nice and attentive to me, and were around so much that they were the only "brothers" I ever had.

As early as I can remember, I fantasized about the family I would have. I imagined that we would be nice to each other, and do things together. My future husband would look at me and smile, and everyone would know that he loved me. People would envy our relationship, seeing how close we would be and how strong our marriage would be. I imagined what my husband would be like. I guess all little girls do. I would fantasize about how he would treat me. How he would care about the little things I wanted, he would never yell at me or make me cry. I knew I wanted him to talk to me, I wanted him to love me, I wanted him to respect me, and I wanted him to protect me.

And I wanted to be like my Mother, in most ways. I wanted to be there for my family like she was. I wanted my kids involved in sports and activities like she had us involved, and I wanted to take the time to lie on the grass and stare at the stars with my kids like she did. I just did not want to be unhappy like she was. My Father had many ways of making my Mother unhappy. I don't know how she coped. *"I will not,"* I told myself. My defenses grew as I matured and began to recognize the pain in her eyes. And, I vowed to myself "I will not be afraid in my own home." My children would not run. They would rest in their beds peacefully at night. *"My children will not be terrorized by a man, any man."* Was the promise I made to myself.

My Daddy was mean. He was mean and he was violent. There were nights when he would argue and fuss for hours, for no reason at all. Even if he had a reason, his rants were extreme and abusive, and usually kept us all up all night. We all walked on eggshells, never knowing what kind of a mood he was in. He didn't physically beat my Mother, but the mental and emotional abuse was just as severe. He would yell and cuss, call everyone foul names, slam cabinets, break things, and make outrageous accusations and threats. And, it would go on for hours, sometimes days.

Our house was filled with guns, and it was a constant fear of mines that he would use one to hurt us. He always had a gun in reach. I remember him making bullets explode on our front walkway. The sound made me tremble, and scared me to the core. He would clean them, and he taught us to clean them. He taught me how to shoot at a very young age. He said we were supposed to kill anyone who would come into our home and hurt us. I wondered if he knew that he was the one hurting us, and that I was prepared to kill him if the day ever came that he would use one of those guns on us. His guns were in clear display in our den. They hung high up on the walls like crown molding.

Anything could set him off and we always had to be ready to run. And I mean that literally, "RUN!"

My
Daddy
and I in
1977.

The roar from my Daddy's Motorcycle could be heard

from the 71 Hwy as he shifted gears and made his way back

home. Something in the roar signaled *"Anger."* My stomach

would begin to turn, and the sensation to urinate vibrated up

though my insides. The slits of light radiating through the

venetian blinds would rested on the wall, and I tried to

concentrate on not peeing the bed. I was afraid. Afraid of

putting my feet on the ground in the dark, afraid of walking on

the cold wooden floor. Afraid of the hallways where my night terrors lived. Afraid of the monsters in the closets that lined the short hallway to the one bathroom in our home. Fear was a constant in my life. The roar got louder as he came closer. I could visualize each corner as he turned it. One, left from the highway. Two, he's making the quick right. Three, he's slowing down at the curve by the golf course. Four, he's idling at the Stop sign by Bailey's market. Five, the roar is louder as he downshifts to make the right turn onto Waters Avenue. The roar now makes the windows rattle. as he turns into our driveway and pulled the motorcycle into his spot at the backdoor.

I listened intently, clenching my little vaginal walls, trying to keep from peeing the bed. I heard the back-door open and shut, and then the sound his Silver Taps on the kitchen floor. The refrigerator door opened and then shut, hard. He opened one cabinet. He slammed it loudly. He grumbled. And I wet the bed.

I slid my wet underwear off under the covers and moved over to the warm, dry side of the bed. My little body curled into a "C" to avoid the wet of my own urine. My eyes are wide open, the covers over my head, only my eyes peering out, watching the lines on the wall made by moonlight glowing through the Venetian Blinds. Lights turned on, the light of the hallway peered under the door. I heard my sister turn in her own bed and sigh.

My Father started an argument with my Mother. Something about how Wanda is turning into a whore, and how Karla has been laying up with somebody. He says he knows this because *"The Streets tell me everything. My own daughters don't respect me, and you the Mother fucker to blame."* I lie and wait.

His rant continued, he was yelling at my Mother. I don't want to hear what he is saying, so I clutch the blankets around my head tighter to drown out the words. They are mean, and they are not true. *Momma has been home with us*, I think to myself. Wanting to yell it at him, but afraid. He is saying that my Mother must be sleeping with the Pastor because she spends too much time at the church. *No, my Mom sleeps here, with us.* My Mother hasn't responded, and so I wait.

I heard his body fall against the closet doors that line the short hallway leading to the bathroom. And then, Silver Taps on the bathroom floor. I can hear the sound as he urinates with the bathroom door open. I pause holding my breath so that I can hear where he is and what he is doing. Then, Silver Taps on the Kitchen Floor, again. I was on the edge of my bed; the wet spot is now cold. I was eight years old and I asked God to stop my Father from hating us. *"Make him nice, God, please? Or kill him. Just, please do not let him kill us."*

He is back in their bedroom yelling at my Mother. *"Damn, Gerald. Can I sleep? I have to work in the morning and the kids have school. Go your drunk ass to bed. "Is* her reply. He is angry, he says. He is angry because his home is all wrong. His wife is a whore and his kids are, also. The other day, I heard my Mother and my sisters talking about the woman he has been spending time with. I wonder if it is that woman whose house he took me to? *She was not pretty, like my Momma* I think to myself. I want to yell at him, *"You are the whore!"* and, I want my Momma to know that we all know that he lies. I don't know why, but he does. I lie in bed and wait. Hoping that he will fall asleep and the episode will end. Sometimes he does, and we are able to fall back to sleep for a few hours, get up and go to school as if we got a good night's rest. Sometimes he does not.

This night, he does not. He cries about how miserable we all are, and how he has to be humiliated in the Streets by how his wife and daughters behave. I know he lies. We all know he lies, but it doesn't matter. His truths are his truths. He continues to yell and cuss. I hear my sisters in the next room. They are getting dressed. I can tell by the exasperation in my Mother's voice, we should get dressed, too. But, I wait. I am afraid of the dark. The front door opens, and I hear my Father on the porch. "BANG!" Gunshot. My body stiffens as our bedroom door opens. Wanda tells us to get dressed, and we do. Fast. I am glad to be out of the wet bed. My Sisters open the second door of our room that leads to the den. And the four of us wait in the den for our Mother. Three more loud "Bang's!" I shake at the vibration of each. My Mother comes into the den, unlocks the back door, and waits. We hear Silver Taps on the Kitchen floor and we go out of the back door and get into the brown station wagon. We are all hoping the car starts. It does, and we pull out of the driveway, make a left on Waters Street, a right on Phillips, and I eventually fall asleep as my Mother drives.

I wake up in a small motel somewhere on the other side of Pomona. My sister washes my face, and changes my clothes. She brushes my hair, parting it through the middle, then braiding two long pony-tails that hang from each side. We pile into the station-wagon and head west. My Mother drops my sisters off near their schools and then turns a few corners and pulls into the parking lot of Madison Elementary School. My Mother and I get out of the car. She goes into the Main office, where she will work as the School's Assistant Nurse. I go to the cafeteria, where I can have breakfast before class. My friends were waiting for me, and I smiled as we grabbed our trays and laugh and talk before the school day begins.

Afterschool, I go to my Mother's office. She tells me it is okay for me to walk home, this means my Father must have calmed down. Many kids are on the sidewalk making their way home, also. As I pass the different houses, I wonder if they are able to sleep at night without being disturbed. I also wonder if any of the kids walking with us have a Father like mine. Then I wonder if any of the kids have a Mother like mine. And I think to myself, as I walk, *"Wouldn't it be terrible if I had a crazy Mother, and a crazy Father?"* And I thanked God, I had my Mother.

My Mother and I at one of my Dad's Motorcycle Picnics.

When I get home, Daddy is asleep in his recliner in the Living room. I go into my bedroom and rest on top of the covers, knowing my bed had not been changed. I fall asleep, and wake up when my Mother come's home a couple of hours later and cooks our dinner. My Father wakes up, and acts as if nothing happened and we all slept in the home peacefully last night. I am grateful. That episode is over.

I always did very well in school. I was an overachiever. My reading ability excelled to the point where I would have to be separated from my class during the reading period and sent to the Resource Teacher to do my own studies. They had ordered books from the Junior High School, and I would be tested separately. I was tested and placed in the Gifted Education Program. My parents would not allow me to be promoted ahead of my grade. I was already a year behind my class in age. My parents had forged a copy of my Birth Certificate to show I was born in December of 1969 instead of January 1970 so that I could begin Kindergarten early. They had coached me and prepped me to have two birthdays. December third was my birthday at school, and January was my birthday at home. I loved it. Hey, who wouldn't want two birthday celebrations!

Popularity came easy for me. I was President of this, and Secretary of that. Dancing and Cheerleading, giving speeches, winning essay competitions, playing the lead in the school and church plays. I was always doing something. I always had a strong group of friends. From early on, I would fight for justice. If someone were being teased or threatened, I would intervene. By Fifth Grade though, I was a little too proud of myself and became more aggressive instead of the assertive child I had always been. I had a group of friends that were smart and cocky. There was my Black friend Margaret, we called her by her middle name Rose so she would be an "R" like the rest of us. Rosie, was from Laos, and Rosa was Mexican. Rayna, Rose, Rosie and Rosa; we were Madison Elementary's own little United Nations. I wouldn't say we bullied anybody, but we definitely were bossy and exclusive. I am sure we hurt plenty of feelings. We were not afraid to fight, and that included boys. We were the best kickball players, and we rode the ropes up into the sunlight. My Mother was the school nurse, and she was never aware that I had become a rogue. For some reason, I could get away with things other girls couldn't. I didn't know why, but I knew that I could.

Getting along at home was not as simple as at school. The tension in our home was elevated all of the time. We lived under pressure, knowing that at any moment an explosion of violence could happen.

It is hard to put into words the danger I felt. But, I mean it when I say that I really thought my Father was going to kill us. I could very easily see us being that family on the news. You know, that family where the man kills the entire family and then turns the gun on himself and then neighbors are on the news the following day commenting about how *"They seemed so normal."* That scenario was very real to me, and I was prepared to not be that statistic. Loving him and hating him all in the very same breath was tortuous for me.

The confliction of my feelings lay in the fact that he was both our greatest threat and our greatest protector. I would pray for God to take him, and then pray for God to heal him when he was sick. I wanted my Daddy, I just didn't want the pain and misery he would cause. I knew he would never let anyone else hurt us, all while knowing that he was capable of hurting us.

From as early as I can remember, until I was in my early teens, there were nights that we would have to sneak out of the house to get away from the violence. Some nights we were able to leave in the car and stay in cheap motels, or at one of my Mother's friend's homes. My Mother didn't have many friends, so that was rare. A few times my Mother would drive us to our Grandparent's home in Pasadena. And sometimes he would show up and act just as crazy at their house as he acted in ours, even his parents walked on eggshells with him. Sometimes, when he wanted to be extra mean, my Daddy would remove parts from my Mother's car so that it wouldn't start. That meant that if we left, we would have to leave on foot, and there were times when we did just that. We would sneak out of the house, hoping he didn't come looking for us. If he did get in the car, or on his Motorcycle, we would have to hide in bushes and duck behind cars, hoping that a neighbor would let us in to sleep the danger away, or until somebody could come and get us and take us somewhere for a couple of days. Things would eventually calm, and in a day or two we would go back home. His rants weren't an everyday occurrence. Sometimes we would go weeks or months without having to run. But we walked on eggshells in the meanwhile, never knowing just what would set him off and always aware that he could snap at any moment.

That kind of home life prepared me early on to fight. I got into fights as a child because I was short tempered and there was so much stress at home, I was not going to take very much away from home. Other girls would tease me with the usual *"She thinks she is cute."* and *"She's conceited."* A time or two a girl followed me home or threatened me at school, and my Dad found out, I had to fight. And I better win. I became a smart mouth in Junior High School. I would debate my point, and raise my voice needing to be heard. I gained the reputation of being loud and argumentative and I continue to be argumentative. Being argumentative and confrontational continues to be something I struggle with to this day.

In spite of our Father's violence, my Mother was a good Mother. I don't know how she maintained a home under those circumstances, but she did. She worked full-time with the

Pomona Unified School District for as long as I could remember. And she was always helping older neighbors, and other people in the neighborhood who were poorer than we were. Our house stayed clean, our yard was always done, and we usually ate a home cooked meal. She kept us involved in sports, and school activities. We went to church regularly, and were usually involved in church plays, clubs and youth groups. I never blamed my Mother for staying, I feel that she did the best she could with what she had. She didn't have her own Mother or family to run to, and people who could have helped were either afraid of my Dad or felt that she chose to stay.

My Mother at Sixteen.

My Mother had been with my Daddy since she was seventeen, and as far as I know had never experienced another man. I remember feeling sorry for her when I was old enough to understand that women want romance and to be treated special by their husbands. Of course, there were some good days in their marriage, but the bad seemed to always outweigh the good when it came to my Father. I always thought my Mother was gorgeous, and I wondered why he didn't treasure her. Beauty was not her only asset. She kept a clean home, she raised us well, she had morals and was decent. I never understood why he seemed so angry with her all the time. And it was no secret that he cheated, and the women he was suspected of cheating with did not compare to my Mother in any form. Funny thing was, he always accused her of cheating. If she went to church, she was sleeping with the Pastor. If she had a good female friend, they were Lesbians. If she had a meeting at work, she was sleeping with the Principle. My Father's accusations were outlandish and unfounded, it didn't even seem that he believed them. His accusations taught me that men are usually very guilty of what they accuse their woman of doing.

I have always been proud of my Mother for being strong. Another woman may have broken under the strain. She could have broken and had a mental or emotional breakdown, leaving us Motherless. She could have killed him, leaving us Fatherless and Motherless. But she didn't, she survived. And more importantly, she led us to God. And so, I learned early on that I could survive. And I learned early on to pray. My Mother remained faithful to my Dad and to us. Always ready when he needed her, and always present when we needed her. My Momma is loyal to a fault, as are each of her daughters. We love hard, long and strong, just like our Mother.

My Mother tried to move us out of the home on three different occasions.

The first time I remember was when I was very young in Elementary School. We moved to an apartment in a nearby city and stayed there for a few months. Another time we moved to an apartment on the other side of Pomona, and we stayed there about six months. That time my Dad fought for visitation with my sister, Trish, and I. Wanda and Karla were older and had a choice, we didn't.

One night, my Dad became violent with me and Trish there by ourselves. We were afraid. He was ranting and cussing, slamming cabinets, and mumbling. We snuck out of the backdoor, went up the hill in our backyard, climbed the fence, and walked along the fence until we go to one of our neighbor's backyards. This was a Mexican family who had lived on the block as long or even longer than we had. Mr. Quiroz didn't want to be involved, but, he felt sorry for us. Trish spent a lot of time playing with his daughter. He agreed to take us to our Mother. We hid in his truck and he drove us to our Mother's house. I was just exhausted when we arrived. Glad to be with my Mom, but, sad because I knew our leaving would cost her when my Dad came looking for us.

My Father came to the apartment arguing with my Mother, and some male neighbors of a Mexican family who lived across the way from us jumped on my Dad. I did not like seeing my Father in that position, I felt sorry for him. We all did. No matter what he did, he was still our Daddy. I think that time my

Mother moved back in with him just so that Trish and I would not have to visit our Father all alone.

Each time my Mother would move us out, eventually, we would bug my Mom to move back to be near our friends or because we grew tired of the financial strain. Either way, we always went back. Over the years the violence decreased, however, my Mother's tolerance of it decreased, as well. The last time she moved away from him, she stayed away over two years. That was during my Junior and Senior years in High School. I would choose to stay at my Dad's a lot during that time so that I could attend Garey High School. It was also a convenient way for me to get my way, I would go so far as to tell my Mother I was at my Dad's and tell my Dad I was at my Mother's so I could have more freedom, counting on the fact that they didn't communicate well.

Because I was the baby, my Daddy and I were closer and he was kinder to me. He had more money, so I received more gifts. And he needed somebody on his side, so, even if I wasn't, I pretended I was and he spoiled me in return. Not to mention, he was probably too tired by then to carry on as he used to. The violence had pretty much stopped completely, so I didn't have to live under the same strain my older sisters had. He would still rant and argue at times, but there was not any more running. And by then we were all old enough to speak our minds, and I spoke my mind a lot. My playing my parents lasted for a while, until they joined forces and created a united front to put a stop to my shenanigans.

One night, during the beginning of my Senior year, I was out with a guy I was dating. He was in College in Irvine and we were hanging out with his cousin and his cousin's girl. My fast ass decided to stay out past my curfew. Figuring I would just suffer the punishment and the lecture when I got home. Usually the punishment didn't stick, and I would be back to my misbehaving. I had a way with my Dad, and after a few hours of coaxing, begging, whining and crying he would often release me from a punishment. Well, that night I got a big surprise. Both of my parents were sitting at my Dad's house when I arrived home. And I had no choice but to move back to my Mother's house. And what made it worse was that they were dating

again. That put an end to my playing both sides against the

middle.

December
1985

1986 Garey
High School
Cheerleader

During my Senior Year, my Father won my Mother back, again. I finally saw him being nice to her, and courting her, and I liked it. She and I moved back in with him after I graduated. My older sisters were grown and having families of their own by then. I was just glad that my Mother would have it easier financially living back in the house with him. And I hoped that my Father would finally love her the way she deserved to be loved.

Through all those bad years, my Mother did not have her own family to run to. I often wondered if she would have stayed with my Dad as long as she did if her family were around. She was estranged from her Mother since her teens. I always thought it was because my Father was Black. Nobody told me that, it just seemed to be the most likely reason. I did not know my Grandmother on my Mother's side. But, My Father's parents, my Nana and Papa, were ever present in our lives, and loved us dearly, so I can't really say that I missed my Mother's family as much as I was curious to know them. Not knowing them never made me feel bad for being Black, I have always felt honored to share two cultures. So, it really didn't hurt my feelings if my Mother's family were prejudiced. I felt it was their loss. We identified more with our Black Culture, anyway, simply because those are the people who were there for us. My Mother even identifies more with our Black Culture. I don't think it's a self-hate thing. I just think it is what it is; she has Black Children. And, I believe that once you have Black Children you gain a better understanding of what it is like to be Black. I tease my Mother a lot reminding her *"You ain't Black!"*

My Nana and Papa on My Birthday.

Confusion and Lies

During my Senior Year, I was infatuated with two men. Sounds outrageous, but it's true. My family had always told me to date and not get "stuck" with one guy like my sisters had. This was the one lesson I took to heart, and to the extreme.

I had met D when I was sixteen, the summer before my Senior Year. He was what we called a *"Baller."* He wanted my sister, Trish, to hook us up and she did. At first, I was totally not interested. I had seen him a few times while I was working at Taco Bell on the North Side of Pomona, and I was not impressed. It turned out that he was related to my sister's man at the time, and she convinced me to go out on a date with him. It took quite a bit of convincing, but, I agreed. D picked me up from my

Sister's boyfriend's house early in the afternoon on a Sunny
Summer Day in 1986

He drove us way out to the South Coast Plaza in his
500SEL. We talked as he drove, and I really enjoyed getting out
of the area. I don't think I had really ever been that far away
from home. He bought as many Fila suits as his arms could
carry. When he asked me what I needed, I replied, *"Nothing."*
The last thing I wanted was for him to think I wanted him for his
money. He was so likable; I changed my mind that very day. I
saw past the *"Baller,"* and thought he was a really nice guy. From
that day on, I was one of his many girlfriends. Now, I did not
know he had multiple girls at the time. And I am not really sure
it would have made a difference, as long as he was not married. I
was not worried about what he did when he was not with me
because he made me feel so good when he was with me, and that
was most of the time. Dwined me and dined me. We enjoyed
each other's company, and we spent so much time together I
didn't think about any other females being in his life.

I did find out he had a serious Girlfriend a few months later. I was pissed when I finally shared my secret with an older girlfriend of mines to be informed that D was very much involved with a woman from the West Side of Town. But, by then it was too late. I was hooked. He was spending most of his days with me, so I never felt deprived of attention. I used my sister's ID to get into clubs and we would go clubbing, almost every week, and he would always make it a first-class experience. We hid our relationship from my parents as long as we could until my nosey sister, Karla, caught us together one day. My family protested our relationship at first, but once they met him, they found him to be a nice guy, also. Even my Mother couldn't help but like him. It really didn't matter to me, it made it easier, but even if they didn't allow me to see him I would have found a way.

Once I started my Senior Year in High School, D would make sure I had a ride home every day. If he didn't come to pick me up he would send someone else to make sure I got home. His many flashy cars created gossip, and I was the talk of the school when his Benz waited outside for me the first time. A few months after school started, I began to feel uncomfortable. I am just not created to be a side-chick. I easily grew tired of hearing the stories of who he was messing with, along with the fact that he had a woman. The Prom was coming, also, and I didn't think that he would be my date. He was twenty-five years old, and although it was cool to have an older boyfriend, I didn't think it was cool to have an old prom date. My Mother did not know he was that old, we had her thinking he was in his early twenties. I began to pull away from D, and decided to date other guys.

Since I had an ID, I could buy liquor and usually did for the school parties and get-togethers. One weekend in December, a friend and I were hanging out with a different crowd than we usually hung with. There was a cute, dark, chocolate dude at my school that I kind of knew, but never really had a good talk with. We talked at the party, and with the help of the alcohol, we ended up hooking up for the night. We didn't have sex, but he put a few hickeys on my neck. This meant I couldn't see D for a long while. It, also, meant my parents were going to go off. And, I was no hoe, so that meant I had to make something more if it then just a *"hook up."* Problem was, he had a girlfriend.

We spent the next few days together, and I put him on notice. He would have to break up with his girlfriend. I didn't like being the side-chick to a "Baller," I was definitely not going to be the side-chick to a High-School Senior! And he did, creating drama between the ex-girlfriend and me. I wasn't really concerned about the drama, though. I was on top of the popularity ladder at school, and I was not afraid of a fight. My parents were glad that I was dating someone closer to my own age. And, it was fun dating someone at school. My parents had no idea of the problems I would soon be facing, what seemed cute and innocent on the outside was far from it.

M and I dated the rest of my Senior Year. Problem was, I would occasionally still date D. And he continued to pursue me. I would resist for a few months, but I just felt so comfortable with D. All it would take is a phone call, and he would come through and scoop me up for a few hours. So, anytime I got mad at M that is just what I did. I loved D, knowing full well that he would never be my man. But, my expectations of D were different than my expectations of M. They each served a different purpose. Dand I were usually honest with each other, and M and I always lied to each other. I guess it was then that I developed my motto, "If I can't trust you, you can't trust me."

I had player tendencies. Point blank. I wasn't honest completely with them or with myself. I just craved attention, and when one wasn't giving I would go to the other. This would go on for the next three years. M being my main boyfriend, and Dand I spending time together whenever we could get away with it. After graduation, I began working and bought a car. Dhad offered to buy me one, and an apartment, too. But, I refused. That would equal my being faithful to him, when he would never be faithful to me. And, I was not up for that.

M and I had a violent relationship. We fought, a lot. I thought that I could fight a man, and I did. I would slap him, punch him, scratch him, and tear up his shit. Eventually, he hit me back. The cycle started and continued throughout our relationship. We would break up and make up; we were more addicted to one another than we were in love. But you couldn't tell us that. It was very unhealthy, but neither of us would stay away from the other.

The violence I grew up with had scarred me. Something about the relationship with M made me feel powerful. I chose to experience that. I wanted to be in that kind of relationship, it was what I expected. Meanwhile, as M and my relationship grew, he was getting involved in street shit. He was spending time with his cousins in LA, and becoming more and more gangster every day. It scared me, and I didn't really know all that he was doing out there in those streets.

I got a call one day that M was shot in the back. I rushed to Martin Luther King Hospital in LA, and his family and I waited for him to get out of surgery. After hours of surgery, we were told he was going to be okay. I never really got the real details out of him about the shooting. What I did know, was that he was robbing somebody when he was shot.

M would continue to hustle on the wrong side of the law, and he would eventually be incarcerated for six months. I visited faithfully, and we talked on the phone almost every day. My phone bills were high, but I missed him. I wouldn't just abandon him when he was in need. Even though, I was not in agreement with his lifestyle. I began to feel guilty, wondering if our relationship had caused him to start hustling in the first place. I wondered if he felt that having to compete with Dmeant he needed to hustle to have material things to keep me. If I had wanted that lifestyle, I would have stayed with D. And that angered me, but by the time I realized it we were too entwined to for me to do anything about it.

In March of 1992, my sister paged me to call home, 911. I called back and she told me that M had been at my house looking for me. I didn't even know he was out of jail. I was out with Dthat day, he and I had been spending a lot of time together, and she suspected it. I rushed home, and got in touch with M. He said he was trying to surprise me. It was more like trying to sneak up on me. I rushed to his aunt's house in Duarte to see him, and we spent the night together.

By mid-April, I was exhausted. I just couldn't seem to get enough sleep, my breasts ached, and every strange sMarcell made me nauseous. Two of my friends and I went to the clinic and took pregnancy tests. Mine's was positive; I was going to have a baby in December.

I hadn't had any real contact with Dfrom Mh to June. I was spending most of my time in Los Angeles, where M was hustling with his cousins. I had caught him in a few lies, and trying to date other girls. We were constantly fighting. So, when D's annual low-rider picnic came up, I went. It was the Pomona event of the Summer. I had to be super fly, so my home-girl in LA boosted (that's shoplifted for those of you who don't know) me some purple suede shorts and a silk shirt. I was cute, and my pregnancy wasn't showing yet.

Of course, D was there, and it was the first time I had really saw him with his main girlfriend. It turned my stomach. I was pissed! I had the nerve to be mad!

A few weeks later, I was so worried and distracted about my pregnancy, that I ran a stop sign and got into a car accident on my way to work. A passerby called my Dad for me and he arrived at the scene when the ambulance was checking me out. My Dad walked up and told the paramedic, *"Did she tell you about her condition?"* I looked up at him surprised, and he finished his statement with *"She's pregnant."* I don't know how, but my Dad always knew when one of his daughters was pregnant. I was actually relieved. The accident had my parents more worried about my health and safety more than they were mad at my being pregnant, and that took some of the pressure off.

My Daddy had my car towed to our house, and he took me to the hospital to be checked out. Once I arrived back at home I called my rescuer, D, and he came the next day with his Tow truck. As we stood on my Parent's porch talking about my car that he was towing to a repair shop, he asked me if I was pregnant. And then he asked me if the baby was his. I told him it wasn't.

My pregnancy was uneventful until one night after eating my friend, Chandra, had to call an ambulance because I had sudden stomach pains. I was rushed to the hospital and kept for three days. They had suspected some type of Heart Condition. I would be rushed to the Emergency Room a second time with the same symptoms and diagnosed with Gallstones. My doctors wanted to wait until the baby was born to remove my Gallbladder. Other than that, after the morning sickness stopped I was fine, as long as I wasn't around any strange sMarcells and didn't eat certain foods.

M and I didn't fight much while I was pregnant, only because we didn't get the chance to. He was out of town too much. We didn't physically fight, but we argued. He had started going up North to Lompoc to hustle. I had moved in with him and his Mother, and he really started being disrespectful. I hardly saw him, and I had suspected him of cheating. In fact, I had proof he was cheating. One day he misdialed my number with his cellphone and I heard his entire conversation with a female. Oh, I was hot! I cussed him out real good, but, it didn't change anything about the relationship. It was still as dysfunctional as ever.

My baby was due December 25th, 1989. I was nineteen years old, in a bad relationship, and having my first baby. M had come back into town anticipating the delivery of the baby. On the morning of December 19th, I noticed that I was leaking water as I showered and prepared for my day. It wasn't a lot of leakage, and I wasn't having any contractions, so I dressed and went to my sister's house. M went to Los Angeles because I didn't think I was in actual labor.

When I told my Mother and sisters that I thought I was leaking water, they made me call the hospital. I was told I had to go in and be checked. When I arrived at the hospital, they checked me. I was already dilated and they confirmed that my water had broken. I was in labor, but I wasn't feeling any pain. I thought it was going to be an easy labor.

Within an hour after arriving at the hospital, contractions started and I had progressed so quickly that by the time I asked for an Epidural, it was too late. I had to tolerate a natural labor.

M came, and stayed with me during most of the labor. The nurse told us that it would be several hours before I delivered, so M went home to change and get our bags. Fifteen minutes after he left, I was delivering the baby with my sister, Karla, in the room with me. Karla softly said, "It's a Boy." When Marcel Rayvonne Gatson made his way into my life and into my heart.

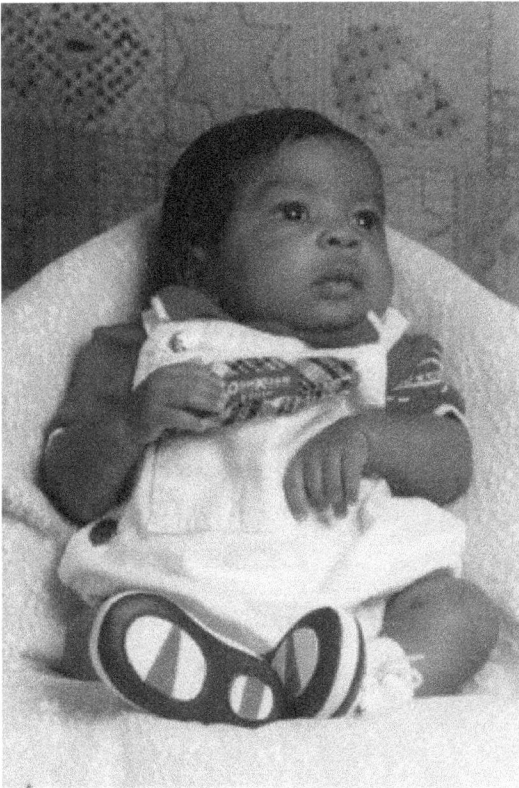

Marcel Rayvonne Gatson, born December 19, 1989.

I held my son and I changed at that very moment. I knew that I had to do better, and be better. I realized that he was totally dependent on me. The awareness that his Father would not be in our lives for long stared back at me from his small dark eyes, and I knew that I would have to step up and make sure he had everything he needed in his life.

A Church Service I attended while I was pregnant came to mind. I grew very subconscious of the fact that I was a young, unwed, pregnant teenager, and I began to feel guilty about how I had been living and the fear of God punishing my baby brought me to my knees. It was prophesized over me on that day my child's Father would not be around to raise the baby with me. It was also prophesized that God knew my heart, and that He still loved me and would continue to do a work in me. That prophecy came to mind at that moment. I hadn't really received it down in my heart before, but as soon as I held my son, I feared that it would come to pass.

Marcel Rayvonne

My son was here, and I had to share him. I wanted him back in my stomach, so I didn't have to share him with anyone. M was present, supporting me for the first few days of our son's life. When we were released from the hospital we took our baby to see my Mother and Father in Pomona, and then we went home to the Condo in Rialto where we were living with his Mother. I felt so out of place. I did not want to be there, at the time I didn't understand why. But, I did not want to share my son with his family. I had no idea at the time why I was so guarded of my son, and why I felt like M's family was a threat. Looking back, it is possible that I may have been disconnecting myself based on the belief that they were either not going to be around anyway, or they would have some power over me and my ability to make decisions for Marcel and I. The reality of being a parent and M and his family having any power over Marcel scared me. I did not want anyone to have that kind of power over me, and definitely not over my child.

M went back up North to hustle a week after we brought our baby home. I was there alone, missing my own Mother, and angry because he had left. Marcel was seven days old when I decided to drive to see my Mother. I packed his baby bag, and put him in his car seat and drove to my Mother's house. My sisters had talked me into going to the Montclair plaza with them for a few hours. I trusted my Mom with Marcel, of course. So, we went to the mall. My Mom called while were there for a little while and told us to come home. My stomach turned flips and I wanted to cry when we drove past the movie theatre and saw D and his girlfriend entering the theatre. I had my nerve. And, my sisters had to keep discussing it all the way home. I was sick to my stomach at the thought, when here I had just given birth to another man's whole baby.

My Mother noticed that my baby's eyes appeared yellow and suggested I call his doctor. I called Kaiser, and was told to take him into the Emergency room for lab tests. I drove Marcel to the hospital, alone.

My baby had to be hospitalized with Jaundice. I stayed with him night and day for four days. M did not come back, and I was very angry with him. When the baby was discharged, I took him back to M's Mother's home alone. I was so angry. M and I fought all the time on the telephone, and when he came to see the baby for a few days I knew that no longer wanted to be with him and I no longer wanted to live there with him and his Mother.

Two weeks later, I took my baby to my Mother's house to spend the night because I was lonely. During the night, I started to feel strange pains in my right side. I woke my parents up because they scared me, and my sister drove me to the Emergency Room at Kaiser Fontana while my Mother and Father watched Marcel.

I needed emergency surgery. The Surgeons removed my Gallbladder and had to explore my abdominal cavity. It was a serious surgery and left me with a huge scar on my stomach. I missed my baby so much. I was so glad that I had went to spend the night with my parents that night. Marcel was safe with them, and I would have been miserable if he wasn't with them. When M found out about my surgery, he told me he was going to get Marcel from my parents. I didn't worry about it. I knew my Daddy was not letting him take my son anywhere. When I called my Daddy to tell him what M said, he confirmed that my son was not going anywhere.

After my discharge, I never went back to live with M. At first the care I needed after surgery was the reason I gave him for not going back to the Condo. Once I healed and told him I would not be going back we broke up, but were still in the cycle of arguing and fighting. He didn't want to let go, even though there was evidence that he had another woman. I tried to encourage him to have a relationship with Marcel and forget about me, but he couldn't.

D came back into my life shortly after I moved back in with my parents. When he found out I had surgery he came to check on me, he was always there when I needed him. The first time he ever saw Marcel he examined him closely. Being young, I thought it was cute. When that situation was far from cute.

We began dating again, right back to where we left off. He gave me comfort knowing that he would come when I needed him, and without stress. I would never talk to D, or fight or argue with him, the way I did with M. Everything about us was calm and comfortable. Everything about M and I was complicated and confused.

Things between M and I turned ugly in March, when M convinced me to go with him to his Mother's house to get the rest of my things. He told me he understood that we wouldn't be together and that we could raise Marcel in peace. I followed him in my car with Marcel. When we got into the house, he changed. I had never seen him like that before. I was afraid, and I knew that fighting back would only make it worse.

M took my son from me, and laid him on the couch. As I went up the stairs to get some of our things he followed me up the stairs. He grabbed me by my hair just as I reached the top stair and pulled me into what used to be our bedroom. My neck snapped back as he yanked my head back. I had never seen that look in his eyes before. I was afraid. And I knew if I fought back, it would be worse. I tried to talk my way out of it. As I fell from the bed to the floor, he stood over me and yelled at me. My son cried as he beat me. Eventually, I was able to try and get out of the room and down the stairs by telling him the baby needed me. He went downstairs and picked the baby up. As I tried to get out of the back door, he ran towards me, laying the baby on the bottom step of the stairs and cornering me in the kitchen. His hands were around my neck, and then he released me and slapped me. My face stung. The baby screamed, and I noticed he rolled off of the step. I tried to get to my baby, but M pushed me away from him and picked Marcel up. I ran to the front door, and left the condo, without my son. I walked down the driveway and found a neighbor washing his car just outside of his garage, and I asked him if I could use his phone. I could tell by his expression and by the throbbing of my face that I showed signs of being beat up. I called the police and I called my sisters.

I reached my sister, Karla, and she was on her way. The police arrived first. They saw my face, and saw M. They tried to talk to us, and I was visibly upset and crying. I wanted my baby, and I wanted to leave. We both displayed evidence of a fight, so the police threatened to take us both to jail. My sister arrived while the police were there, and we were able to talk them out of taking anyone to jail. The police convinced M to give me my son, and I was able to leave.

My sister took Marcel home with her because of the circumstances. She asked if I wanted to go home with her, but I just wanted to be in my own bed and I went home to my parent's house. I was exhausted and just wanted to sleep. At that point, I wasn't even trying to hide the fight. There was no way I could hide it at that point, and I was too mentally drained to even try. My Mother began to lecture me as soon as she saw me, but stopped when I told her I would never be with him again. My Father, he didn't react the way I had expected him to. We didn't realize it then, but he was too ill to react.

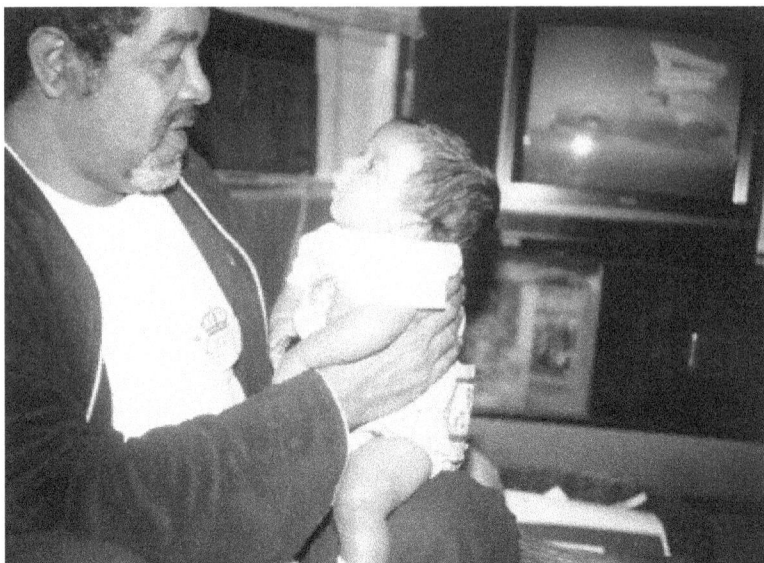

My Dad holding Marcel, January 1990.

Prophecy Fulfilled

In spite of our fight, I wanted Marcel to have his Father in

his life. M barely helped, and whenever he did come to see him it

seemed as if he were more concerned about me than he was

about the baby. I was not able to relax around him, and

struggled to take responsibility for the part I played in the

violence without discounting the fact that no matter how it

started, we had both been victims of abuse. It would be years

before I was able to process the fact that I had abused him, and even harder to accept that I had been abused. Rumors were spreading that M was not my son's father, and I fed into them. Telling M that he wasn't, so that he would leave us alone, and I could get on with my life. M's Mother was caught in the middle of our violence. I knew she loved Marcel, but I was angry that she seemed to not be concerned with the abuse. I felt bad cutting her out of my baby's life, but it seemed necessary to put an end to the cycle of violence.

Marcel's first year seemed to fly by. I learned quickly that I wanted and needed more stability in my life than a High School Diploma would offer me, and I decided to quit working full-time and start taking College courses at Chaffey College. I found a part-time job and my parents helped with Marcel, my Dad was especially attentive to him. He would hear him cry and come into my room to get him. My Daddy would feed him and change his diapers during the night so I could sleep. I would feed my baby boy his dinner, bathe him and put him to bed and my parents would watch him if I wanted to go out. My friends and I would club in the Inland Empire usually, and sometimes out in

Los Angeles. My parents didn't mind my going out, and sometimes my baby would stay with my sisters. For a while, M would show up somewhere looking for me, and he even waited on my block for me to come a home a few nights. But, I was determined to separate myself from him, and eventually he stopped trying.

By Marcel's first Birthday, it seemed that M was accepting that we would not be a couple. I gave Marcel a big first birthday party, but M did not attend. He did come and see Marcel the following day on his actual Birthday and it was a friendly visit. For a moment, I believed that we might be able to co-parent successfully. Everything changed, when later that day M was arrested and he was facing years of jail-time. The prophecy was being fulfilled.

Treat Me Right

The Club wasn't crowded. It was our usual hang out spot, Wednesday nights at Fantasia. We didn't wait in line. While I usually dressed upscale to party, I was casual this Wednesday night. I hadn't felt like partying, I was tired and just was not in the mood. My girl, Denise, had practically begged me to hit the club with her. For some reason I agreed, even though my young son, work and school had me exhausted. I pulled my hair into a ponytail, put on a little make-up, a silk blouse and my jeans with the leather down the front. We pulled up, parked and walked into the club. Greeting the doormen and saying "Hello" to acquaintances as we passed by. We never had to wait in line, and as usual, we walked straight to the entrance and into the club.

We were standing at the bar, taking shots of Jose Cuervo Tequila when I noticed him looking at me. He was cute. Not too tall, a little thick like I like them, and he had a baseball cap on. *"Hmmmm, how did he get in here with a cap on?"* I wondered to myself. Trac and Denise noticed our eye contact, and dared me to approach him. We laughed and teased for a few minutes and then I walked over to where he stood.

Treat Me Right, by Chubb Rock was playing. We danced and he continued to eye me; showing me he was interested. I flirted back. I was definitely feeling him. We danced a couple of songs, and then walked off the dance-floor to talk.

His name was "Kenny". Kennith Michael Moorer, to be exact. He was visiting from New York, in California to see his brother. He came to Cali a lot. *Okay, that's good*, I thought. *I'm tired of these California brothers anyway*, it was time for something new. We exchanged numbers. He was staying in Fontana, not too far from Pomona, where I stayed with my parents. And he was only going to be in town for a few days.

I had recently gone back to College, and I worked part-time nights at a security company doing dispatch. My days were filled with school, work, and my one-year old son. He didn't seem worried that I was a young Mother. He asked if I would see him the following day. I went home excited, fantasizing about this small seed of romance that had been planted.

The following day, I went to see him where he was staying, at his brother's house. His brother and wife were not home, so I didn't meet them that day. We went to see a movie and picked up some chicken from Kentucky Fried's Drive Thru on the way back to his brother's home. We sat, we ate, and we talked. And he tore up those wings! We were compatible. He made me smile. He seemed nice enough, and I was intrigued with his New York accent and his conversation. I had that feeling that I would know him. That he would be a part of my life. Everything just felt right.

On Day two, I parked my car and he let me in the house, he turned and kissed me on the lips. *He must have been thinking about that all night*, I thought. It was a cute gesture, and I was glad he did it. We sat and talked some more. I had to use the restroom, and he showed me where it was. He sat in his brother's room, waiting for me to come out of the restroom. I thought that was a little strange at first. But then, he pointed to a large poster his brother had hanging on his bedroom door.

"Who is that?" he asked me. I looked at the poster, *"It's MC Lyte."* I said, thinking, *"Duh, it has her name on it big as day.* *"No, who is that?"* he asked pointing to the young man standing at MC Lyte's side. I looked closer. *"Is that you?"* I asked. *"Yeah, that's me."* And I was introduced to his alter ego, DJ K-Rock. Just

as much as it intrigued me, it scared me. I could only imagine the life of a DJ, being on the road, traveling from place to place. It didn't scare me enough to pull back, but I was on notice that he lived the Hip-Hop Lifestyle. And in my mind, that was *groupies, parties, and more groupies.*

I found it quite strange, that a week earlier, a young rapper from Compton had called me to ask if I would ride with him in the Compton Martin Luther King Jr. Parade. Mix Master Spade, (R.I.P.) and I had met at the Palladium a few months earlier and had become friends speaking on the phone often. We weren't dating or anything, we had just become phone friends. When I refused to ride in the parade, Spade commented that, "*I heard you go with DJ K-Rock.*" I didn't know a DJ K-Rock at the time, and told him so. But here I was standing with him a few weeks later. It was puzzling, and I never figured out what had given Spade the impression that I was dating K-Rock. My best guess is Kennith was eyeing me for some time, and had spoken my name somewhere at some time or another. Kennith still can't explain it.

Me in 1991, around the time Kennith and I met.

Kennith left a few days later to return to Staten Island, New York. He assured me that he wanted to keep in touch, explaining that he visited California often for shows and that we would be able to see each other often. The coming months would include letters, cards, and long telephone calls. I knew from the moment I saw him that I could love him and I did.

My parents had about fifteen hissy fits when the phone bill came. Kennith's phone bill was double the price of mines. We spent thousands of dollars on phone bills. We spoke every day. We talked about everything. He traveled often, and I loved that he was seeing the world.   I thought it made him more mature and cultured than the rest. We would talk each other to sleep at night, and then wake each other up in the morning. I looked forward to seeing him again.

It would be almost exactly one month later that he would be in LA for a show with Lyte. He was staying at the Hyatt on Sunset. I drove to LA after work, and met him at the Hotel. Being hugged by him was the best feeling ever. It felt like home, like he was where I was supposed to be. I felt safe and I felt protected. We made love. It felt like I had known him always, like he was made for me. We blended together so well. I think the distance between us put a rush on things. We saw each other as much as we could this trip. He stayed a couple extra

days, and in between our schedules we squeezed in time for each

other.

Daddy

My parents were concerned about my new relationship.

My Daddy was always suspicious of men. He asked a lot of

questions, the main one being *"Does he have a job?"* And I was

ecstatic to tell him about Kenny's career. My Dad was sick by

this time. We didn't realize that it was Cancer that was thinning

his frame and weakening him. My son was the highlight of his

days. Looking back, I realize that it was because my Dad knew

he was dying. As badly as they didn't want me to have a child at

nineteen, my son was a blessing to my Dad. And if I hadn't had

Marcel then, my Dad wouldn't have known any of my children.

As my Dad's health declined, Kenny was there for me. He

listened and he was becoming the man in my life. I didn't realize

that I would lose my Dad so soon. In April of 1991 my Dad was

hospitalized and given six months to live. Years of abusing his

lungs with cigarette smoke had caught up to him, and he had

Lung Cancer. We brought my Dad home with Hospice, and made a schedule to keep up with who would be doing what and when. My Mom had to continue to work to keep my Dad's Health insurance effective. So, my three older sisters and myself took turns providing care.

Being the baby of the family, I had always been exempt of having to take care of family business. Not that I was not capable, I was just last in line. This situation was a shock to my whole world. I couldn't be the baby anymore. Starting a relationship at this crucial time in my life may have contributed to my dependence on Kenny. I can see that with the wisdom I have now. At the time, I was just thankful to have a man that was growing into the role that my Daddy was passing over to him. It was just a natural progression. It was not intentional, it just happened. As my protector sailed away, I saw Kenny drifting closer on the Horizon and it gave me peace. He would have to take on the role that was left vacant.

I waited for my Mother to arrive home from work, so that she could assume the duty of caring for my Dad and my young son. My Dad's condition had declined daily. It had only been about a week and a half since we had received the six-month prognosis. His confusion was worsening, and he appeared thinner and thinner each day. I had made him lunch this particular day, and he wasn't able to feed himself. It made his dying so real to me. I was alone with him, and I didn't want to be. I wanted somebody else to come and take over, but there was no one else that day. I wanted to scream, and I wanted to cry. My Dad couldn't feed himself, and so I fed him. Spoonful by spoonful, it was agonizing.

My Mother came home and I left for my evening Psychology Class at Chaffey College. I drove with tears in my eyes for what seemed like a long time, on a route I had taken for months. Suddenly, I didn't know where I was. I was lost. *How could I be lost going someplace where I had been so many times?* I pulled over, and I broke down. I sat in my car, on a street in Alta Loma for about an hour.

I returned home that night, exhausted. I called my Professor and left a message on her voicemail. I gave my son a bath and put him to bed. I didn't tell my Mom about my day. She would worry, and she had enough on her plate. While I was studying, my Dad walked into my room. He was so weak and frail. He leaned on my dresser and he talked to me.

My Dad stood in my room, leaning against my dresser and he told me. *"Don't let them get you. You have to be strong, and don't let them make you weak, because they will. You're going to be a good nurse."* Although his words were garbled, it made sense to me. He had raised me to speak my mind, even though he didn't want it spoken to him. He taught me that not every adult was right, and that I could question an adult. He taught me that not every teacher was good, and not every minister on the right. He told me that I could speak up, that I was a person, and that I didn't have to listen to what was wrong. I believe that is why I was never abused sexually as a child. No matter who told me not to tell, I would have told my Daddy. He raised us to be on alert. He told us that nobody should touch us, we weren't allowed to hug or kiss relatives or grown-ups. I believed that my Daddy could protect me from anything, all the while knowing he was my greatest threat. With all of his negative ways, he did instill important character strengths within his daughters.

I talked to Kenny that night. Never sharing exactly how I was feeling about losing my Dad. I went to sleep late, and Marcel slept unusually well that night. My Mother knocked on my door the next morning. *"Get up, I need you to go and check on your Dad. I think he passed."* I began to protest, and started to cry, but she stopped me, *"I need you right now. "I* saw in her eyes that she really did need me, so I tried my best to hold it together. I told her to call my sisters, I wished one of them were there so I did not have to be the strong one, but they were not. The knocking woke Marcel up in his crib, and my baby stood there watching me, waiting for me to pick him up.

I walked into the room next to mine, where the hospital bed had been set up. My Dad was gone. I knew immediately. He was not cold though. I looked at my Mother standing in the doorway and shook my head. My Daddy was dead. I had begged God to take him some nights during his rants, and now he really was gone and I wanted him to come back. I begged God for a few more weeks, a few more days. I wasn't ready. *I want to take care of him some more, this is the first time he was nice. I'm not ready for him to be gone. Why did you take him right when he was changing?*

I knew he had willed himself to go, and I even wondered if he took too much medicine intending not to ever wake. The day before was the first time he was ever incontinent, and then he was not able to feed himself. My Dad had always said he did not want to live like that. I was thankful that he had softened; thankful that we got to see a side of him that was calm and almost nice. He had even prayed with us, and so I believe that God took him to Heaven. I didn't think that he was intentionally horrible to us. I think he just didn't know any better. And I think the Korean War took his mind.

I went back into my room and picked my son up out of his crib. I took Marcel into the room where my Daddy was and stood over him. I didn't want him to feel alone. Marcel wanted his Grandpa to hold him. He leaned over and wiggled out of my arms and into his Grandpa's bed. He sat and looked, waiting for his Grandpa to hold him as he had so many times before. I cried, wishing that my Dad had spent more time being the man he was for those few weeks after his prognosis. My son was sixteen months old when my Father died, and I had just turned twenty.

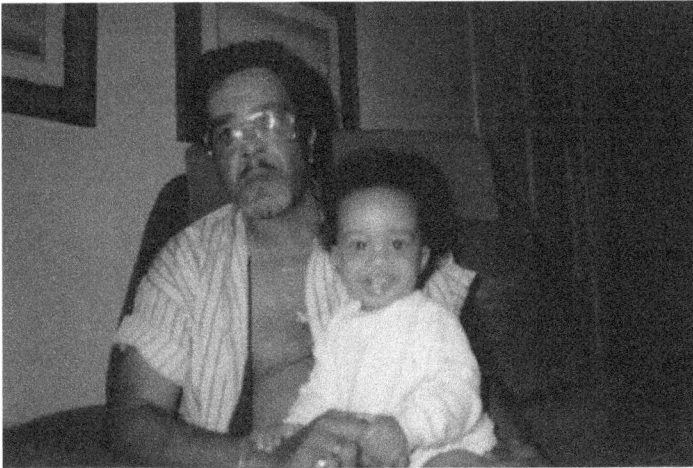

My Daddy with Marcel in the weeks before his death in 1991.

My sisters and their families arrived in waves as we waited for the paramedics to pronounce my Dad and for the

Funeral Home to pick him up. Seeing our Father taken away zipped up into a body bag was hard. Especially because there had been many times when I prayed for God to take him.

My Dad's Funeral was held. Kenny couldn't be there physically, but he called often and supported me as much as he could from far away. D was there for me. He came and escorted me and Myles to the funeral. It felt good to have him there. We weren't romantically involved at the time, but he cared about what my family was going through. But, he had been close to my family since I was sixteen. I loved him for his consistency. He was always there when I needed him, in fact, he still is. He knows me well, and he has always respected me. I was thankful to have his support through my Dad's death.

The past has a way of coming back and forth throughout life. And my Daddy's funeral was not exempt. The repast was held at our house, and when it was almost over I overheard my Mother and older two sisters talking about a woman that was there who was supposed to have been my Daddy's oldest daughter. Apparently, one of my Dad's aunts had brought her. I became angry knowing that someone came under false pretense. I was not angry at her coming to the funeral, I was angry with her for coming to our home and not introducing herself to my Mother. I felt it was disrespectful to stand by and watch us without our having knowledge of who she was. I have no idea who she is, what her name is, or the circumstances of how she is supposed to be our sister. I asked my Mother why she didn't tell me when the woman was in our home, and my Mother replied, *"Because you don't know how to control your attitude."* I wasn't interested in knowing who she was then. But, if it would help her to talk with me or know me, and she contacts me, I will be open to meeting. We never heard from her again, unless my family kept that from me, also.

Long Distance Love

Mother's Day followed the next week, and Kenny sent me flowers and he also sent my Mother flowers. I was impressed. My love for him grew each day and I became more and more attached to him, even from long-distance. He had begun to call me using calling cards, and I would have to go to phone booths to receive his calls so they couldn't be traced. Young and naïve, I didn't stop to think of the repercussions. We just had to talk every day, and that was all that mattered at the time. He continued to travel and see the world, and I continued with school, work and raising my son. Eventually, I would be laid off of my job. Then collecting unemployment when I could, with welfare and food stamps helping to provide for my child.

With my son's Father, M, being incarcerated, it made it easy for me to bond with Kenny. He showed concern and support to my son. Kenny would help me financially, and that bonded me to him even more. I appreciated him so. I was glad that his parents were still together. He seemed family-oriented; especially when he talked about the love and connection he had with his Grandmother in Alabama, and his aunts, uncles and cousins. It made me feel more comfortable to know how important family was to him. He seemed concerned about me, and he had adapted well to being the man in my life. We talked about almost everything, and I trusted him.

I trusted him to be him. Of course, I wanted him to be faithful to me, but I doubted it. I had never known any man to be faithful. So, I was looking more at his other attributes. As dysfunctional as it may sound, I expected men to cheat. I knew I could not be there with him, and just as I was vulnerable, I knew that he was. All that mattered to me at the time was how he treated me. How he loved me, and how he loved and treated my son. I was glad for the time we had together, and I tried not to worry about the rest. I knew he loved me, and I felt that anyone else was just to occupy his time and nothing more.

Kenny and I in 1991.

Marcel and Kenny would meet later in that year. Marcel took to him fast. Kenny stepped right into the Father role. It was like God had sent him right to us. I was so happy. For Marcel's second birthday that year at the end of 1991, Kenny bought him a motorized Jeep. It seemed as if everything I was looking for, was in Kenny. He loved us, and I loved him deeply.

Kenny and I
in California
a few months
after we
began dating.

Kenny would send cards, and flowers often. Once, he had

a friend of his who spoke Spanish leave a long message on my

answering machine. I don't speak Spanish, even though I am

half-Mexican, but my Mother does. My Mother had to listen to

the message and interpret for me. I thought that was so cute.

That man was doing everything right. I just knew he was made

for me. He would make several trips to California that next year.

Surprising me at my college once, and surprising me at my house another time. We grew in so many ways.

MC Lyte was one of the artists hired to work at Disneyland's Grad Night that year. This meant that the entire crew would be staying in Orange County for at least a month. Kenny and I would get to spend a lot of time together. So that June, Kenny was near me. I visited often. He would keep Marcel, wanting to spend more time bonding with him. He took him to Disneyland, and his friends and the rest of Lyte's entourage got to know him. Marcel was like a little Mascot. Wherever Kenny went, he was there. Marcel called him "Daddy", and Kenny ate it up.

Kenny, Marcel, and I in the apartment in Anaheim during their weeks performing at Disneyland's Grad Nite.

We would laugh and talk in the apartment. The other guys would have girls there, sometimes. But, it was like a big, happy family, and I had the car. So, they liked having me around to run their errands, and get them places. One night we all went to Roscoe's Chicken and Waffles. Lyte and I were courteous to one another, but I wouldn't say we were friends. I am sure she met many of her crew's women, and until she started seeing me often, I could tell she became more courteous. I once had to drive her to downtown LA to rush and get a passport. Other than that, we really only had a "Hi, how are you?" interaction, nothing deep.

They had to perform multiple nights a week, and the money seemed good. K wasn't complaining. I had begun to call him "K" around this time. We spent many nights together, one in particular, we made love in the Jacuzzi of the apartments they had temporary housing in. It was exciting and fun.

One evening, in January, before my twenty-first birthday, I came home from my night class at Chaffey College to see a car parked out front of my house. I didn't recognize it and as soon as I opened the door, there was Kenny to surprise me. I was so excited. He brought me this big bomber jacket with Lyte's logo on the back matching his. And he brought Marcel a shirt with Chuckie airbrushed on it, and the front said, "Rayna N Kenny's Lil Chuckie". I was touched. He wanted us to be a family, and he was doing everything right to show me that I could count on him.

We went to Fantasia that night, together. The DJ's shouted us out. People who had knew me since forever and knew him, told me that we were both good people destined for blessings. We were sitting to the far right of the club, I was sitting on a high stool, when Kennith turned to me and hugged and kissed me. He whispered in my ear. *"We met here."* And he paused, then said, *"Do you want to get engaged here?"* and he had a ring in a black box. *"You think we gonna get married here?"* I was smiling from ear to ear. I had no idea he was going to propose. I was super excited. He put the ring on my finger and they announced all over the club that we were engaged. People congratulated us. It was all so cute. I loved the way he did it. My Mother told me that she could see that he loved me in the way he looked at me, and that made me happy. We took pictures that week, the three of us. We were the family I always wanted.

Our Engagement Photos.

Kenny had my loyalty. I saw me when I looked at him I

had absolutely no doubt in my mind that he was my future. I

wanted to be his partner, his helpmate. I knew that I could trust

him with my heart, and I put my walls down. I didn't expect him

to ever make me afraid, like I had been most of my life. I began

to feel safe and secure, and I wanted to give him all of me. He

was the man with whom I could finally rest.

The Past and The Present

"I have something to tell you." Kenny sounded like

he was in some sort of a dilemma over the phone. Those are the

worst words ever; they don't prepare you for anything good. It's

always bad. Well, it wasn't that bad, it was unexpected, but not

really bad. "This girl I used to date is coming around now and

saying I have a daughter. She is like 8 months old. It was before

you. There was some question of whether it was mine or not.

But, yo, she looks just like me." My heart dropped. He went on

to explain who the girl was, how this all went down, and what

his plans were. He was spending time with the baby, his family

accepted it, and from the photos he would send, she did look like a lot like Kenny. *"Okay, well, we can do this"* I thought, *"Now we have two kids to provide for, but we can do this."*

No doubt I had Kenny's back. I wanted us to be a family, his, mine and ours. We would make it work, and I vowed that I would love his just as he loved mine. It was strange; I would get a funny feeling when I would hear the baby in the background. I couldn't help but wonder if he and the Mother were really over. But, I was intent on being supportive. Kenny and the baby girl's Mother would argue at times over this and that, but I stayed out of it. I just wanted everyone to get along, and wanted what was best for the kids. I encouraged Kenny to be a good Father, and I knew I would treat any child in the way that I wanted my child treated. I looked forward to meeting my stepdaughter, and playing a positive role in her life.

I would get a funny feeling when I would hear the baby in the background. I couldn't help but wonder if he and the Mother were really over. But, I tried to be supportive. They would argue a lot, according to what he would tell me. There seemed to be a lot of miscommunication. I encouraged him to not just be financially supportive, but to be there for his daughter, and from what I could tell, he was.

In January of 1992, I flew to New York with Kenny. It was my Birthday present. I stayed at his parents' home, him in his basement and me in the room upstairs. It was a nice trip. I stayed from the fifteenth to the twenty-first.

We flew into JFK, and I remember getting off the plane, it was freezing cold and the first thing that came to mind was, "It's so dirty!" I had never seen snow before, and the black snow was just disgusting to me. Kenny had his cousin, Cynthia and her husband, Anthony, pick us up from the airport. She was big and pregnant with her second child. And they seemed like a really nice couple. They drove us to Staten Island, New York where Kenny's parents owned a home. Kenny's parents had given me permission to stay there, in a spare bedroom upstairs. Kennith's room was downstairs in the basement. Kenny had one sister who by then lived on her own and his brother Kenny's big Brother in California. Alfonso, the eldest brother had died as a pre-teen he was hit by a car while riding his bike. I met his parents, Prisilla and Jesse. They seemed nice, they loved one another and his parents were still together. That gave me hope that Kenny would want a long and happy marriage.

We had so much fun. Kenny and Lyte performed at the Apollo Theater and I remember standing on the stage during sound check and looking around thinking, *"I am at the Apollo!"* That was the same weekend the movie *"Juice"* came out, starring Tupac. Tupac was also at the Apollo that night, and we were introduced. Who knew he would become one of the most widely known rappers of our generation. I've never been one to pull a camera out, or become a fan when meeting industry people. But, that is one occasion when I wish that I had.

While I was in New York, I answered Kenny's phone and a female sounded upset and asked who I was. I replied by asking her who she was, after all it's only polite for callers to introduce themselves when placing a call. She told me that she was his *"fiancé"* and continued to ask questions like *"Where is Kenny?"* and *"Who are you?"* My response to her was *"If you are his Fiancé, you should know where he is and who I am."* I have always had a smart mouth, and always been quick to respond. The call ended, and it messed with my head a little bit. I rationalized it with the fact that I was there, and she wasn't. I didn't think Kenny was being completely faithful to me, but I felt that it was because of the distance that was between us. Years later, I would find out that she came to the house while I was there. Somehow, Kenny was able to keep it from me. Apparently, he was more than unfaithful. He was engaged to us both at the same time. Honestly, I don't think it would have made a difference had I known then. I was so in love with him, and believed that he treated me better than any other female, so I probably would have stayed thinking that it would all change when we were living in the same state.

I went home after five days, more in love than when I had arrived, in spite of the telephone call. This was when I began to seriously consider my moving to New York. I was ready for change. I wanted to experience something new, and I was in love. I knew I would miss my family, but it was also an opportunity to do some new things and live a different life. I had grown tired of the life I was leading in California, I was tired of the men, and the hustlers I had grown accustomed to dating. Kenny afforded me an escape, and I was willing to uproot my son and relocate. I have been told by friends who have known me for years, that I was also "Most Likely to Move to New York and Marry a Rapper." So, in a way, it seemed like my destiny.

Kenny's big brother, and I had developed a friendship during those first years. He lived near me, and it turned out we knew some of the same people. He and his wife had suddenly separated, and it saddened me because they had seemed happy. Reggie had bonded with Marcel, and acted like he was his Uncle. He would ask for me to stop by with Marcel often and we would talk. Kenny's big Brother liked me and shared a lot of the family's past with me. I learned that he had not been on speaking terms with his parents for some years. I was determined to judge Kenny's family on my own experience. If I had learned anything from growing up in my own household, it was that we never really know what goes on behind closed doors. Every family has problems, and I just hoped their problems were in no way like the problems I had grown up with.

Later that year, Marcel and I would take a two-week vacation to New York. Kenny and I had been together a year and a half by then. Marcel would be introduced to Kenny's family, and I would be meeting his daughter. It worked out well. His daughter was adorable, she looked like Kenny, was built like him and everything. I took to her quickly. She had a sweet spirit. Kenny's family took to Marcel. He was welcomed into their home, and they treated him well. Kenny's sister, Kenny's sister, was nice to him, and she had a son about two years older than Marcel. So, it was beginning to feel like we would fit nicely into their family.

We enjoyed New York, taking Marcel on the Ferry, and into the city. He was only two and a half, and small for his age, but he seemed to enjoy himself. Kenny bonded some more with Marcel, he was the only Daddy Marcel knew at the time. God was blessing me with a man who loved my son as if he were his own, and I was grateful.

Kennith and I at his parent's home on Staten Island, New York, 1992.

That vacation sealed the deal. Kenny's parents were moving back down South in the fall and Kenny would take over the Mortgage payments on the house in Staten Island. We would live there together. I was excited to begin my new life with the man I loved.

Kenny and Lyte had a falling out that year and K stopped working for her. I never knew what really went down, but I always knew there were two sides to the story. Kenny does not talk a lot, especially about things that bother him. But, life kept on pushing, so we had to keep our plans moving along. Kenny's parents were packing up and moving to Alabama. His Mom, who had been diagnosed with Parkinson's disease a few years earlier, was retired. His Dad had just retired from NYC Corrections with a healthy retirement income, and they wanted to move back to the South to be near Jesse's Family.

Kenny's Paternal Grandmother, Uncles, Aunts and Cousins all lived around Bay Miette, Alabama, which is close to Mobile. Kenny's parents had talked with us and the plan was for us to take over renting their house from them and K was to pay all utilities and upkeep. Kenny hadn't saved much, so he needed a job if he wasn't going to DJ for Lyte. He continued to DJ locally, but needed a steady income for his daughter, and for my son and me.

K applied for a seasonal job with the US Postal Service. And he got it. It was hard work, especially during the winter, and then again during the hot weeks of the summer. But, he did it. He eventually was hired on permanent, giving him a good benefits package and steady income. We bought our plane tickets, and began preparations for our move. Marcel turned three in December of 1992 and we celebrated his Birthday/Going Away party at My Mom's house. A few days later, we boarded a plane to begin our new lives in Staten Island, NY. Just in time for our First Christmas together as a family.

Saying Goodbye

Marcel's party was fun. Marcel was turning three on December 19th, and we were flying to New York a few days later. My friends and family were all at the party. Kenny's big Brother, and three of Kenny's cousins who were visiting from New York were even able to come. We ate and played games with the kids, I bought him a huge piñata shaped into a clown. It was so huge that when filled with candy we could barely lift it off of the ground. I tried to enjoy the day without thinking about how much I was going to miss my family.

My Mother and I were not getting along at the time. I know she was scared for me. And I was overwhelmed, I perceived her as being negative and expecting the worst when I was trying to stay positive and expect the best. I was moving across the country with my young son, and it must have been as overwhelming for her as it was for me. Because we weren't getting along, I had moved out of my Mother's house to stay with my friend, Miko, in an apartment that her Father owned. My sister, Trish, needed a car, and so I planned to leave my car in her care with the agreement that she would pay the remaining car notes, and the insurance. Everything was falling into place for our move. I had packed and sent boxes ahead to New York. Everything else, I either packed or gave away.

M's Mother hadn't had much contact with Marcel over the time period that he was locked up. She kept him overnight a couple of times, but I didn't let her take him to see M in prison. She had tried to give me a money order at one time when M had first gone to jail, but I refused it because she didn't sign her name. She had signed M's name. I felt as if she was trying to establish that he was providing for Marcel, when he was not. I didn't want my son exposed to jail. And I did not want him exposed to a female that had called and threatened me over the phone. M would call me collect, telling me he still loved me and wanted us to be a family. Then, at other times, he would have someone call me on a three-way call and he would be rude and cuss at me and talk crazy to me. I figured out that he was trying to impress some chick on the three-way phone call. So, one day he called and I started reading a letter he wrote me saying how much he loved me and wanted us to work things out. Sure enough, the female hung up the three-way call and called me back threatening me. I wasn't having Marcel exposed to any of that. I was ready to live a new life, I wanted to be free of M, free of my past, and free of that volatile relationship.

I contacted M and we planned to meet at the Montclair Plaza. I wanted to meet in a public place, to avoid any arguments or fighting, and I had a friend there with me to watch and as proof that we had met. M and I talked and it was actually pleasant. He was able to see Marcel and interact with him for a while. M didn't seem surprised that I was moving. He said that he would like to remain in contact with Marcel. I asked him if he would sign his parental rights over, and he refused. His refusal was the last connection to my son, and I was glad that he didn't cut that last tie.

Leaving Home for Home

Marcel rested his head on my chest as we flew across the country. I was eager to be with the man I loved. We were finally becoming the family I had always dreamed of. As I pushed Marcel's stroller through the airport, my stomach ached. I wondered if I was doing the right thing. I didn't want to live with a man before being married, but I didn't think our relationship would have survived if we didn't make it happen. I rationalized it by the fact that I did have a ring on my finger. *"At least we are getting married."* I told myself.

Kenny was excited. I saw it in his eyes and in the way, he moved that day. I watched him closely, looking for reasons to believe in us. I would not speak my fears out-loud. I wanted to believe that we would be the ones to make it to forever. I rested my arm on the middle armrest, enjoying the gentle touch of his skin as he drove us home. I looked out of the window, asking God to forgive me for shacking up, and rationalizing my sins with all of the ifs, ands and buts that swirled through my head.

I bathed Marcel and put him to bed. After showering I unpacked some of our things and tried to absorb my new atmosphere. Kenny seemed happy. He talked more than usual, and he smiled a lot. The noise of Staten Island was very different from the noise of Pomona. I stared out of the window at Vanderbilt Avenue. It didn't feel like home. It only felt like home when Kenny touched me. I lay my head cradled in Kenny's arm and stared out the window listening to the sounds of Vanderbilt Avenue. As he held me I prayed for my family and fell asleep.

I woke eager to be a good little pretend wife. I got up early and energetically and made Kenny and Marcel breakfast. It was cold outside, and the floor heater made strange noises. I watched my son eat, and wondered when he would realize that this was *"Home."* Having to dress for winter weather was tough for me. I told myself that I would avoid going out unless absolutely necessary. I bundled Marcel up, and bundled myself up, and the three of us went to the market. The A & P Supermarket was different than the grocery stores in California. Kenny introduced me to Potato Bread, and packaged Jamaican Beef Patties. It felt good to shop with my man. Anxiety always has made me talk a lot, and we talked and played through the aisles of the A & P. We held hands, and took turns pushing the cart with Marcel in it. Then we went and got a pizza and went back home. I was glad that the grocery store was close to home. I did not look forward to driving in the snow.

398 Vanderbilt Avenue, the house where
Kennith grew up and where he and I
would bring two of our own children
home to.

We pulled into the driveway of what would be our home.

Our driveway was on an incline, and as I got out of the car I

slipped on some ice and fell all the way down the driveway. It

was hilarious. I laughed, and Kenny laughed harder. I knew

getting used to New York would not be simple. There would be a lot more falling down, and a lot more getting up in my future.

The first few days I focused on unpacking our things, and making the house more comfortable for Marcel and me. Marcel was my company when Kenny went to work. Cleaning and reorganizing kept me busy, and I was glad I didn't have to go out in the bad weather. Kenny would take the bus to work early in the morning and I would eventually venture out on my own to learn the Island. Trying to be the best *"wife"* I could be; I started taking Kenny lunch in the afternoons. I was intent on being the partner he needed and the woman he wanted.

In the evenings, we would play Spades or Backgammon for fun. Taking care of my son, and my man was my priority. I told myself that if I took care of them, they would take care of me and all would be well in my world. And I was a good little wifey. Kenny's uniforms were pressed and hanging for him every morning. The house was clean, and dinner was cooked. I did everything from massaging his back to cutting his toenails. I wanted him happy.

I was not happy, completely. My heart ached for my Mom. I had never been away from her for so long. The choice I had to make didn't seem fair sometimes. The first month was tough. Kenny was my man and I was very happy to be with him, but I needed my Mother. I needed my sisters. I missed my nieces and nephews. My Mom and I talked almost every day on the phone. The price for love seemed very high. I debated myself almost daily. Weighing the pros and the cons of love. *"It will all be worth it."* Was what I told myself when I cried in the shower.

The more I ventured out into my new world, the lonelier I felt. I had never been so isolated. I could walk past hundreds of people, and not know one person. Not have one person say *"Hello."* There would be days when it was just Marcel and me. Kenny worked a lot and spent time working on music in his basement. I wanted to see more of New York. Kenny wasn't very interested, and it surprised me. His disinterest in my asking him to take me into the city was the first thing I didn't like, but would have to accept. I understood that our money was short, but it didn't feel like that was the only barrier. It hurt my

feelings, and that made me feel guilty. Kenny was the only one

working, so I stopped looking for entertainment. I focused on

what my family needed, and pushed aside what I wanted.

Telling myself, *"If I sacrifice today, it will pay off tomorrow."*

Baby Steps

The first time I rode the Ferry after moving to Staten

Island, I was alone. K's cousin watched Marcel, and I journeyed

into the city looking for employment. As I stood below the

terminal waiting to board onto the bottom of the boat, I was

proud of myself. *"Little Pomona Girl in the Big City"*, I thought to

myself with a smile. I sat on the boat and watched the people,

wondering what kind of story each of them had. It struck me

that most of them looked unhappy. There was a rush in the air.

Nobody appeared to be enjoying the commute. "I must look like

a tourist sitting her smiling", I thought to myself. And I stopped

smiling.

Getting from the Ferry terminal to the first subway train was simple, I was supposed to switch trains beneath the World Trade Center. I got off of the train and looked around, trying not to look like a tourist. It was overwhelming. I had never, ever been in such a busy place. The environment was motivating. I was getting a chance to see things, and do things that I had never imagined. I never imagined moving away from my family. When I was little and I fantasized about my future I thought it would be in California near my family. But, this, this was exciting. I looked around and tried to find my next train by following the signs. I was lost. And I didn't want to miss my appointment. After wandering amongst the crowd for about fifteen minutes, I decided to ask a cop. Thank goodness it was a nice cop, he showed me how to get to my train, and I was on my way to my first job interview.

The interview went well, and I was hired! My very first interview, and I got the job. I celebrated by grabbing a slice of pizza before I got back on the ferry and returned home. Kenny was at the Ferry terminal to pick me up, and I kissed him soon as

I got in the car. Things were working out, and I saw God blessing me in spite of my sins.

The small Nursefinders office was comfortable, and my three co-workers were very nice. I was trained quickly to manage the phones, applicants, scheduling, and interviewing the Nurses the company used to fill private duty and per-diem nursing positions. I wanted to be a nurse, and just being in the environment made me feel closer to my goal. The commute was fun, even though the weather was still cold. City life was appealing, when I got my first check even going to the Bank in New York was a new adventure. I ventured into the city streets every lunch hour. I loved shopping in the small gourmet markets for fresh salads and sandwiches for lunch. There was a vendor booth in front of my job that had the best curry chicken and rice, and one across the avenue that had the best hot dogs. I bought Marcel a new toy from a street vendor every week to make him smile. The business of the city helped me to not feel so lonely.

All I wanted was pizza. Day and night; pizza. I craved it. When I missed my period, I knew why. I was pregnant, and pizza was my one desire in the beginning. I was overjoyed, and I bought a card and wrote in it to tell Kenny he was going to be a Father.

Kenny was excited. We had his daughter and we had Marcel, and a new baby would be the addition to make things perfect. Kennith's daughter was so lovable. I loved her, and she loved me. She and Marcel got along well when she visited us, they would play and share, and our little family was happy.

Two months later, the small office where I worked was given notice that it would be closing. We would tie up all the loose ends, and close the office in July. It worried me that I would be pregnant and un-employed, but there was no changing what was already in motion and I promised myself that I would enjoy my pregnancy. I had prayed, and prayed hard for a daughter.

Kenny and his Baby's Mother began to disagree about things. Kenny was feeling that she was keeping his daughter from him. I was not sure if my being around had anything to do with her pulling the child back, it didn't seem to bother her when I first moved to New York. I tried to stay out of it, while supporting Kenny and encouraging him to be actively involved in his daughter's life. Kenny decided to request Court-Ordered Visitation from the courts. When he had her served, she was angry and wouldn't allow him to see his daughter.

As the weather warmed, sitting on the front porch was like an adventure for me. Our street was active, Park Hill Projects was only three blocks away and the Bodega and shops were right around the corner. One day we sat on the porch enjoying the day when one of his daughter's Cousins came and sat with us. Surprisingly, as we all talked he told Kenny His Baby's Mother had another man thinking he was the baby's Father, also. This was shocking. Especially when the cousin also told Kenny that it was very likely Kenny was not the Father.

Several weeks later, the courts would order DNA tests. I didn't doubt that the little girl was Kenny's. She looked too much like him, and we all had a connection with her. She felt like she was his. Kenny's voice was shocked as he told me by telephone that the baby was NOT his. He was angry, and we were sad. He talked about suing her for all his money back, but he didn't. I told him to let that go, encouraging him to continue to be in the little girl's life. My being pregnant did not fill the void that losing that little girl left. I still wonder about her, and hope that she is happy and healthy.

Family, Friends and Adversaries

After the company, I had been working for closed, the loneliness came back. I prayed asking God for more friends. When Kenny's sister, called and told me that she and her friends were going into the city for a night out, I had to pause and swallow when her next question was asking me to watch her son. I hurt my feelings that she didn't ask *"Do you want to go and hang out in the city with us?"* I knew immediately she would not be a friend to me. My feelings were hurt, but I watched her son, anyway.

I would end up watching her son, a lot. And she would hurt my feelings, a lot.

I longed for a sense of family, and I always felt that family should help each other. And so, I became her babysitter. Our house became her Laundromat. And she became my adversary. Kenny's parents would make extended visits, sometimes staying for three to four weeks at a time. They are very critical people, especially his Mother. I had painted the inside of the whole house, and when they came to visit and saw the paint job her first statement was, *"What about the floors?"*

Her son spent most of his time at our home. I would pick him up from school, do his homework with him, feed him, sometimes I would bathe him, and sometimes he would even spend the night. I thought that her job as a Corrections Officer caused her to work long hours. It would be several months before I would realize I was being used.

Kenny's sister wouldn't come get her son immediately after she got off work. She would go home, relax, change, sleep, and come at her leisure. Later, I would find out that she would even go and spend time with her friends before picking up her son.

She would use her key to enter our house whenever she felt like it. As if her parents still lived there and we were not tenants.

Kenny and his sister have a strange relationship. Sometimes they act like they are best friends and other times they can't stand each other. I never witness Kenny doing anything to Kenny's sister, it's usually Kenny's sister manipulating her way into Kenny's life. Kenny's sister is allowed to say and do whatever to whomever, with the excuse of *"That's just how Kenny's sister is."* Kenny would tolerate her until she pushed him over the edge and then he would explode and say something. I thought Kenny should tell his sister about the way she treated me. He didn't. I would have to speak up for myself.

I felt very uncomfortable around any of her friends. It felt like I was under a microscope being examined. It reminded me of high school, when you have a friend who doesn't want you to mingle with her other friends. I could feel the tension.

Kenny and Big Regg in front of their parents first Pensacola, FL

Around November, K's Brother came to town. He had changed jobs, sold his house and started providing security to Lyte. I could see this troubled Kenny. He felt left out. And I thought he wanted his brother to help fix the situation, and not just be on Team Lyte while K was on his own. K had been developing his studio in the basement and it was slowly coming together, but I could tell he really missed being in the spotlight with Lyte. Kenny's big Brother drove his truck to Pensacola, and left his huge dog there. And then drove his Red Nissan Mini-truck to Staten Island. The plan was for him to stay with us when he wasn't on the road with Lyte.

I would hear Kenny's big Brother talk to Kenny his faults for the Lyte situation. Lyte had another DJ, and I hurt for K. Lyte and DJ K-Rock had been a team since they were in their teens and it just didn't feel right. I didn't comment. I tried to be as supportive as I could be. I admired Kenny so much. Seeing him work hard out in the snow, walking and delivering mail. He was respectable, and I loved him so much for working so hard for us. I knew that there were many young men who wouldn't have done it. And I was proud that my children's Father was a man who would do whatever he had to in order to provide for his family.

Regg and I would sit in the Sun-Porch where our TV was and have long talks. He would tell me about the problems he had with his parents when he was growing up. He told me that he always felt like he wasn't given the material things or the opportunities Kenny's sister had been given. He seemed to resent his Father. I didn't realize that they had gone years without speaking until he told me so. I was glad that they were speaking again, and that he would be around for the birth of our new baby.

Kenny's big Brother spoke up about the way Kenny's sister treated me. He saw that she was rude and abused me as a babysitter. One night, Kenny's big Brother knew that she was at her friend's house while I was at home not feeling well with the pregnancy. He told her about herself. And he encouraged me to speak up and not tolerate her abuse. I loved having Kenny's big Brother in our home; he was the Big Brother I never had.

Cynthia and I continued to spend a lot of time together. We would pool our resources and help each other out. She would babysit for me, and I would babysit for her. If I had a chicken, she would make all the sides and we would have a good dinner for our families. Cynthia taught me hospitality, and she taught me a lot about cooking. The closer Cynthia and I became, it seemed the harder Kenny's sister worked to make me miserable. There started to be discord among the family, with Cynthia in the middle being accused of treating me better than she treated Kenny's sister.

Baby Love

The first day I went to apply for welfare, I arrived at nine in the morning and the line was down the street. By the time I got to the door, they were not taking any more applicants. The next morning, I arrived at seven thirty, and still was not first in line. I sat in the Welfare office watching the people around me wondering about each of their stories.   I lied on the application, of course, pretending I did not live with my baby's Father. Technically, Marcel was not Kenny's, so that helped in obtaining the benefits. We were struggling financially, and I needed some type of insurance to get prenatal care.

I was diagnosed with Gestational Diabetes and had to learn how to check my Blood Sugar levels and give myself insulin shots. It was another High-Risk Pregnancy meaning I would be seeing the Doctor twice a month instead of monthly. As the pregnancy progressed, I would have to go to the clinic at Staten

Island University Hospital weekly, and then almost daily during the last month. Kenny was attentive and he went to doctor's visits with me sometimes when he was able to get the time off.

I was obsessed with feeling my baby move in my stomach. During one of my Ultrasounds, we were told that we were having a girl, and we were both very excited. I had to have ultrasounds almost daily near the end of the pregnancy, so we saw that it was girl early on. I wanted to name her *Raquel*, but Kenny was not having that. Then I suggested *Shayna Jazmine,* and we agreed. We prepared for the birth of our daughter. We even went to Childbirth Preparation Classes, we were a team and everything felt right. He was attentive and loving, and that helped me to adjust to being so far away from everything I knew. The best moments of those months were when we would lie in bed at night and he would hold my belly with Shayna kicking him reminding us of what was to come.

Kenny worked hard to get the things we needed for our baby. We shopped together, and planned together. Cynthia hosted my Baby Shower and Kenny's sister did not come. I was glad she didn't come. I never want anyone who has ill feelings to celebrate with me. I felt badly for Kenny, though. I expected her to at least come in support of her Brother's child.

Kenny's big Brother was at home the morning I left for a Doctor's appointment. He watched Marcel, and I drove to the clinic next to the hospital alone. It was January 26th, 1994. I went into the Ultrasound Department, and waited to be called. When the technician left the room, and came back with one of the Doctors, I thought something was wrong.

My amniotic fluid was decreasing, and it had decreased so much that I would have to give birth soon. The doctor told me I would be induced. I was taken to the hospital's labor and delivery unit. I called home to tell Kenny's big Brother that I was being induced and I needed him to find Kenny and tell him to come to the hospital and Kenny's big Brother would watch Marcel. I had left a message for Kenny, but told Kenny's big Brother to make sure his job knew I was going into labor.

The nurses had made me comfortable and put the Cervidil in to soften my cervix. The room was quiet, and dark when Kenny peeked around the door. His presence brought me peace. He leaned down and kissed me on the lips, and I smiled. Our baby was coming, and it was just he and I, and that was enough.

The Cervidil was supposed to help the cervix to thin and efface. It was a slow process. Contractions started late in the night, and came on steady and strong. Kenny reminded me to breathe and focus, and I did. I tried to tolerate the pain, thinking that I wouldn't be in hard labor any longer than six to eight hours. Marcel's labor was over in six hours, and I did that without an epidural, so I thought that my second baby would come easier and faster. I was wrong. After six hours of hard labor the nurse came in to check me. *"You are partially effaced and dilated to two."* She took her gloves off and washed her hands. I looked at Kenny with tears in my eyes. It hurt like no other pain I had ever experienced in my life. It felt like my hips and my ass was going to come out of my vagina.

Kenny rubbed my back as I lay on my right side, trying to take the pressure off of my lower back. He was very attentive and involved. It was comforting. The Nurse gave me some intravenous Demerol to relieve the pain because I the doctor was concerned that I was too tense and my body was not allowing the labor to advance as quickly as it should. The pain medication allowed me to sleep for a few hours, but I didn't feel rested. The pain medication caused some crazy dreams.

When I woke up Kenny was asleep on the couch in the room and the room was dark. I called the nurse in and she checked me again I was dilated to four. I begged for an epidural. Kenny held me as I leaned over to allow the Anesthesiologist to put the epidural in my spine. He was there every moment of labor, and I appreciated it.

At five fifteen in the morning on January 27, 1994, I was delivering our daughter; Shayna Jazmine Moorer was right on time. As she was born Kenny's watch alarm was going off as it did every morning. She was beautiful. A head full of black hair, almond shaped eyes and pointy ears Just like her Daddy. My baby lay on my chest and Kenny and I just stared at her. She was everything. I was so in love with my little family. My hopes and my dreams were in my reach.

Family Life

Our new baby girl was buckled safely in her car seat as we made our way home. Marcel was so excited to see his sister. Kenny had the house clean and smelling good. He had even cooked. I had a calm in my spirit. There was a peace in my soul. My kids were able to rest at night, and we didn't have to run. I had the family I had always dreamed of.

Kenny was so good with the baby. He learned how to care for her and she seemed content when she was in his arms. I tried not to be lonely, and I tried not to miss my family. I was a little lonely not having many people come to the hospital or come to our home. But, I convinced myself that I only needed Kenny. I told myself that it was okay. *"All you have to do is focus, this is your family. And it is enough."*

Kenny had a good friend, V, who worked as Lyte's Security, and was also an aspiring Rapper. He and his girlfriend, Kim, moved in around the corner from us. They were renting out Dee's house. Kim was from Philly and we became fast friends. She was cool and down to earth. We spent a lot of time at my house, especially when V was out of town with Lyte's entourage. I was glad God had sent me another friend.

Cynthia and Anthony were great cousins. I appreciated them so much. Sometimes I felt guilty, like I was wearing out my welcome. They were everything for me at times. And I leaned heavily on them. Eventually, I would meet Monique. Monique knew Kenny's big Brother and Kenny and she reminded me a lot of me. She was outspoken, strong and opinionated like me. Monique had a daughter about Marcel's age and I would begin to spend a lot of time over her house. I finally started to feel like Staten Island was home.

Having two young children kept me busy. And Kenny and I didn't have much romance going on. Money continued to be tight, and time was limited. There was no extra money for me to be cute, and I fell into a rut. Jeans and a t-shirt was my daily attire. I didn't feel sexy. And I didn't look sexy. Getting my nails done, or my hair done was not priority number one. Every other need in the house came first. I didn't know how to do it all. I chose to have a Birth Control device implanted in my arm. It was supposed to keep me from getting pregnant for five years. The mood swings and weight gain was terrible, but we didn't want any children any time soon, so it seemed like a small price to pay.

Kenny and I in the year after
Shayna was born.

I continued to push my feelings aside in order to cook and

clean and raise my kids. I really thought that women were

supposed to be able to do everything, and I believed that taking

care of myself was selfish. I thought, *Women are supposed to*

sacrifice. I didn't know that in order to take care of everyone

else I needed to be at my best. I expected the most of myself, and I wore myself out trying to be everything Kenny, Marcel, and Shayna needed.

Shayna at six months old.

Kenny introduced me to a girl on his mail route named Syeda. Syeda had a son about a year older than Marcel, and she stayed home to provide care to her sick mother. We hired Syeda to babysit the kids once I found a job. She would watch Shayna all day, and take Marcel to school in the morning and pick him up after school with her own son. I felt comfortable; she was loving and kind and took great care of my kids. Syeda and Monique had been friends for years. Meeting them widened my circle as they introduced me to their friends and family.

I found a job in New Jersey working at a Bottled water company when Shayna was a couple of months old. I enjoyed it. We needed the money and I needed to get out of the house. It was hard leaving my baby daughter, but part of me was relieved to have time away from home. With both of us working full time and two small children, Kenny and I weren't spending quality time together. I missed him. I began to miss the way we once talked, and the way we once played. I began to feel a disconnect from him around this time.

Regg and I would sit in the sun porch where a TV was and have long talks. He would tell me about the problems he had with his parents when he was growing up. He told me that he always felt like he wasn't given the material things or the opportunities Kenny's sister had been given. They had started speaking, just before Kenny's big Brother moved back to New

York, and I thought that was great. This was my new family and I wished everyone would get along. Especially for my kids' sake. Kenny's big Brother would Introduce us to his new girlfriend a few weeks later. He had met a young lady while Lyte was making a radio appearance at a radio station in North Carolina. Kenny's big Brother told me that he was in love with her. I asked him what he loved about her and he told me she was kind, and supportive, and secure. She was younger than Kenny's big Brother, if I remember right, she was younger than me, and I was twenty- two at the time. I cautioned him. He had told me she had a young daughter. And yet, either he was there, they were in New York, or they were out and about traveling with Lyte. I questioned him, and I advised him, sharing my concerns with him, *"Where is her child when she is out and about all the time with you? You know I don't leave my kids for days like that. And if she works all week and spends all weekend with you, where is her child?"* Kenny's big Brother became defensive and told me that her Grandmother takes care of her daughter and that is what family is for. I agreed, *"That is what family is for, but a child need her Mother. And it doesn't seem like she spends a lot of time with her child, and that concerns me."*

Kenny's big Brother told me he was going to marry MD. We also talked about her having an ex who didn't seem to want to let her go. Kenny's big Brother didn't seem concerned about the ex, and I didn't think twice about it. Lots of women have problems with an ex-boyfriend when the try to move on. A few days later Kenny's big Brother left for North Carolina. I spoke to him on May 4th, when he told me about the ad he took out for the newspaper asking Madupe to marry him. I thought it was romantic and sweet and wished them the best. I hoped they would move to New York. I wondered about his ex-wife. She still loved Kenny's big Brother; you could see it in her face. I knew she would be hurt. We were never close; we spoke rarely and would run into each other on occasion when I was in California. It didn't feel right, but Kenny's big Brother seemed happy and he was a grown man capable of making his own choices.

IRREPLACEABLE

I answered the phone to a loud moan, someone was crying. "What happened? Priscilla, what's wrong? Are you okay? What's wrong?" I heard desperation and terror in her groans. Priscilla was crying, she was sobbing, and trying to speak. "Reggie's dead! He's dead! Reggie is dead!" she finally got out.

"Wait, no. Who told you that? I just talked to Reggie last night. Who said that?" I asked, trying to rationalize. "MD called, she was crying and she said Reggie is dead." She said through her screams and sobs. "Okay, where is Jesse?" I asked. "He is on his way home." She moaned. "Okay, stay by the phone. I am going to find Kennith, he should be here soon. Just sit down and call me back if anybody else calls you, okay? I'm gonna find out what is going on." I didn't want to cry, I didn't want to break down, then I couldn't get the answers I needed. "Damn!" I yelled, I didn't even have MD's number; I had no idea where they lived, no addresses, and no names. Hell, I didn't even know her last name. I called Kennith, no answer. I paced, and then I thought to look on the phone bill, I knew Reggie had often used the home phone to call North Carolina.

K walked in the door, he immediately knew something was wrong by my face. I started to break down, I cried. "Kenny, you Mom called. Something's wrong." He interrupted me, "What's wrong with Ma?" he said preparing to drive to Pensacola. "No, somebody called her, MD called her and told her that Reggie is dead." The cries broke through. "Naw, get the fuck outta here. Who said some shit like that, Who playin'." He didn't want to believe it. "Your Mom is freaking out, you Dad needs to get there quick." Kenny called his Mom and talked to her. He hung up the phone and ran out the front door. "Oh, my God." I cried some more. I don't know what the kids were doing, but they were quiet. I looked for the last bill in the drawer and found it. I scanned it for North Carolina numbers; I called the number I saw most often. It rang three times. "Detective" she said her name, but I forget what it was. Her voices sounded like she was a black woman. I tried to speak very calm and matter of fact. "Hello. My name is Rayna Moorer. I am hoping you can please help me. I am in New York. My husband Is Kennith Moorer, his parents are Jesse and Priscilla Moorer, they live in Pensacola, Florida, My Mother in law received a phone call that her son had died. That is all we know. Please help. I don't know what to do, where to go, who to call." There was a pause, she asked me to repeat my name, telephone number, and the family names, numbers and locations. I did. "I will have someone get back to you." She started to say, I interrupted her. "Please, ma'am. We need to know something. We don't know those people down there. My brother in law lives here with us. He is down there visiting his girlfriend and we get a call that he is dead. Please, please what do I do? If we drive down there where do we go. Something must be wrong for a detective to be answering the phone. I don't even know where I am calling; I just called the most frequent number in North Carolina on my bill. Please help me." She paused again, "Well ma'am I am a detective. I am on a crime scene. There has been a murder." My heart dropped. "Is it Reginald Moorer?" I asked. "We can't

identify the body as of yet." She said. "Oh, Reggie is about 6'4",
and over 300 pounds, brown complexion, short hair, big feet.
Does he have an ID?" I questioned. "I'm sorry ma'am, yes. He
has an ID with that name, and he fits that description." I inhaled,
telling myself not to breakdown. I needed info. She gave me her
name and number, the station number, and told us to call her if
we arrived in Greenville.

I sat and cried. I waited for K to come back. He did, with
his neighbor friends. I told him what the detective had told me.
We were blessed that she was helpful. K's parents went to
Greenville on the way back to New York. It was very strange that
Madupe and her family were allowed to identify the body and
have it released from the Coroner. By the time his parents
arrived he was in a Mortuary. MD called me, and we would talk
on the phone at times. She cried, she wanted to vent, she wanted
to see if people hated her, thought she was to blame.

Kenny's big Brother was shipped back to Staten Island.
He was in a local morgue when his ex-wife arrived. She stayed
the night with us. She looked heartbroken. She didn't talk much,

and she didn't seem to want to hear about the last few months. I wondered why Reggie had seemed to uproot so fast, and make such drastic changes in his life, but we didn't talk about it. wanted to see him and she wanted to see him alone. She went to the funeral home, and spent time with him and that she was able to tell him all that she had to say. She appeared to be so heavy with emotion. I felt so badly for her. She didn't attend the funeral. She said she wanted him in private, and I can understand that. I still can't help wondering if he would still be here had he not left his wife. Looking back, the whirlwind of change signaled something was going on. He was just moving so fast. Oh, how I wish he were here. He gave me a sense of security. It wasn't just his size; he just would do anything for my family. I often wished he were here for me to talk to. And I really wish he were here to be an Uncle to my kids.

IT JUST DON'T SIT WELL WITH ME

The funeral was hard. A lot of family came up from Alabama. I tried to make everyone feel welcome. It was so overwhelming. I was so young, and I pushed my own feelings aside because he was their blood and I saw everyone around me hurting. All I knew to do was to be strong, and try to make things easier on everyone around me. The grief, the sadness, my kids, everyone else's kids, and Kennith's grief was hard to watch. I hurt for his parents; they had lost their second son. I could already see them becoming overprotective and overindulgent with Kennith. Many people came to the funeral. The repast was at my home. I didn't go to the gravesite. I had Shayna and I wanted to go back and get the house ready for the guests. Kennith had to leave the funeral when the viewing began; it was too much for him. I noticed a young woman run after him. I was already on my way to check on him. She hugged him. And then I comforted him. He hurt so badly, only God got him through that day.

At home, the guests began arriving. MD's family came. Everything just felt strange. Like I was in a dream. Friends visited, family stayed. I was just spent. I couldn't believe that we were really burying Kenny's big Brother. My daughter was in her baby swing and I was sitting near her on the stairs. The house was full, and I noticed the same young woman who had ran to hug Kenny just staring at my daughter. I watched for a moment, and I found it odd that she didn't smile at her; she didn't say any of the customary baby talk greetings. She just stared, and it wasn't a stare of admiration.

As the guests began to leave, there were a few stragglers. It was then that I overheard K's Aunt talking with the same female and introducing her as *"Kenny's ex-fiancé."* *"Oh, ok. That must be her."* I thought to myself. *"No problem. She's paying her respects, but she better not look crazy at my baby again."* I thought to myself. I picked my daughter up and went to sit on the porch. K was sitting with me when she and one of Lyte's dancers who I considered to be my friend, came onto the stairs, to say their goodbyes and leave. K got up so they could walk down the short staircase leading to the walkway and leave. A while later when the phone would ring. I answered, it was one of the dancers asking for Kenny. I could hear the female talking in the background and I swore she said, "I just want to talk to him". I paused. "Look, I don't appreciate you bringing her here and nobody letting me know who she is, yet she's walking around my house talking about she's Kenny's ex-fiancé. I think that is rude, not to mention the way I saw her staring at my daughter. She didn't bother to say hello baby, God bless her, or nothing. Now, she has you calling under false pretense so she can talk to him? Y'all tacky." He was silent, and then he did what I didn't expect him to do. He said, "I'm sorry. I in no way ever meant to disrespect you. "And then he passed the phone to her, who tried to explain that she just was concerned. My response. "Yeah, you're concerned. Be glad today was about Kenny's big Brother. Disrespect me again in my house, and I won't be so nice." And I handed the phone to Kenny.

In the coming months, I would have several telephone conversations with MD. She would cry, tell me how much she loved Kenny's big Brother. Tell me about her ex and how he abused her. She told me, and showed me the ad where Kenny's big Brother proposed. The more she talked, the more confused she sounded. She told me how she hated her ex and she knew he was responsible. But, then she told me that she met up with him to get her cable box back so she could turn it in to the cable company. Then she told me that she still had mail going to his address, which we knew for a fact because we found recently dated mail with is address on it in Kenny's big Brother's truck. K's parents were in contact with the Detective, and they were seeing how MD's brother played a huge role in setting Kenny's big Brother up. It all just really started to make me sick to my stomach. At first, I wanted to comfort her, but then I just wanted them to stop the lies. Kenny's big Brother was tricked, thinking that he was marrying into a good family, when they were just full of shit. And then, her sister, who lived in the apartment where it happened, moved back in there. That just didn't sit well with me. Nothing about it did then, and nothing about it does now. I just stopped talking to MD. I had to, I think she could tell I was irritated by her, and I believe she could tell that I was no dummy. We stopped communicating. They took my brother, and my kid's Uncle. They took K's brother, and they took a part of him on May 5th, 1994. I believe it was February 1995, when I would see her on Television, as a guest of the Montel Williams Show.

She was looking for a Valentine's Day Date.   Talk about

disgusted. Later, revelations in court and in transcripts would

describe many people involved in the case including her brother

who called Reggie and told him to leave the door unlocked so the

paid Hitman could take his life. Kenny's big Brother was

murdered in exchange for Two-Thousand Dollars, if I remember

correctly. Senseless.

THE LIES SHE TELLS

Kenny's sister wrote the obituary and created the

programs for the funeral. Of course, I wasn't mentioned. But

even worse, Marcel wasn't mentioned. I guess it's true that some

believe blood is the only determinate of family.   It was just

another one of her tacky insults. I found comfort in knowing that

Reggie loved Marcel. They had a bond. And he considered

himself to be Marcel's uncle. He spent a lot of time with him,

especially when we were still in California. Nobody can take

time and kindness away from you, nobody.

Reggie's arrival in Staten Island was the beginning of me putting an end to being used by Kenny's sister. ehad spoken up for me, and now that he was gone I would continue speaking up for myself. I saw that no matter what I did, no matter how much I did, she was just not a respectful person. I began to see that she was confused. People on Staten Island would ask me if Kenny was Puerto Rican. When I said no, they would comment that Kenny's sister is. Kenny's sister hung with Puerto Ricans, and she spoke Spanish. But her Momma and Daddy are from Atmore and Bay Minette, Alabama. No Puerto Rican Blood to be found. This was amusing to me. Several people told me that she actually told them she was Puerto Rican. Later, I would realize it's really more sad than amusing. *"It's really sad that she doesn't love herself enough to be herself."*

Many of Kenny's sister's friends attended the funeral, friends who would get their first glimpse of me, and the inside of my home. This was the unraveling of Kenny's sister's attack on me. It would come later, but here is where it started.

MISSING CALI

In 1995, we took a family trip to California. I had left my car in the care of my older sister, Trish. And I was angry because our agreement was that the car stay in my name, she was to pay the insurance, and the rest of the car notes and she could keep it. Well, I found out that my Mother paid the note off because she wasn't paying it and my Mom was the co-signer. And then the insurance lapsed. I wanted my car back. Kenny the kids and I flew to California and we took the kids to Disneyland. I was able to visit my Mother, who I missed terribly and the kids were able to spend time with all of their cousins. It was a good trip. Kenny and I were able to spend some time together. Seeing my family was just what I needed. Kenny and his friend, Tony, drove the car back to New York and the kids and I flew back.

My Mother and I in front of
the home where I grew up
on Waters Street in
Pomona.

I had not had a lot of contact with my friends from

California after I moved. And when I vacationed there it seemed

as if all my time was occupied with my family. I had built up

resentment for some of my friends who didn't seem to try to

keep in contact with me. My feelings were delicate, and I took

lack of contact as lack of love. I made an effort to reach out to my

friends, and not all of them made an effort to reach back.

I missed my family very much, but I wanted to live in

Staten Island. I liked the experience. My family life was not

good, but I had faith that it would come together. I felt that K was my partner in life, and I was dedicated to having our family together. I would visit Cali often. At least once a year, I am sure my Mom worried about me. My family usually expects the worst before welcoming the best, so I was watched closely when I was home in Cali. I would cry so hard when I had to leave and go back. It was so hard to be away from my Mother, from my family. I knew that my kids had a big support system in Cali. Only one of my sisters, Wanda, ever visited me in New York one time. My niece, Summer, came and stayed for a few weeks one summer. I had three of my friends that came to visit me at different times. I often resent that my family wasn't more supportive. I wish they had been able to visit the kids and I more often. My oldest niece, Summer, did come and stay one summer with us. She babysat for me, and I paid her in school clothes. I wanted to do much more with her and take her into the city, but money was tight. Kenny's sister did offer to take her into the city. I allowed Summer to go, even though I wasn't invited. My brother-in-law, Marvin, came to visit once when he was in town. And a good friend from high school, Tuesday, came to visit. She had family in Brooklyn, and was able to spend a few days with me when Shayna was a baby. I loved seeing my people from California, the visits were rare but greatly appreciated. My best friend, Miko, came and stayed with us for a few months. She rented a room to be close to the city and pursue her dancing.

Kenny and I the night he gave my
25th Surprise Birthday Party.

My twenty-fifth birthday came, and I was going to dinner with Monique and Syeda. Kenny was at home watching the kids.

We were almost to the bridge when Kenny called and told me that Shayna had a high fever. We rushed back to my house, and I ran in expecting to check on my sick daughter. I was surprised by a house full of people. Kenny had thrown me a surprise party. I was so emotional, I cried. And we had a ball. We ate and drank, and ended the night with our usual cake fight. Kenny and I would always have a cake fight. At the end of the night there was cake and frosting from the dining room to the kitchen down the stairs and into the basement studio. We had romance that night, I felt loved and wanted.

I Quit

In 1996, I was still working for Echo Springs. I had witness the Comptroller of the company, Cecil, abuse and harass other employees. He would write notes that looked like he broke the pencil grinding it into the paper, and these notes would contain insults, derogatory remarks, and threats. I watched him do it to drivers, office employees, and even the owners. I knew that he had to have something on them to get away with it. I began to compile a file, saving his notes he had written to other people, writing down dates and times when he would rant and cuss in the office. I thought I could help someone by keeping notes. And then the tables turned on me. I had assumed additional responsibilities of someone he had chased out of the office. He started leaving me notes, but, I would walk into his office and discuss things with him. I was not going to be bullied. We all began to discuss why he was able to do such wrong and get away with it. He simply had the owners by the balls. He had dug himself so deep into the financials of the company that the owners needed him because they were not devoting the time necessary to stay on top of things. So, Cecil was the only one on top of things. And the company was in the process of going public. Well, I gave my resignation, and two week's notice. That was when Cecil began to use one of the managers to harass me. He would talk to me because I would talk back, so he would have Ed do his dirty work. Ed would be very nice, he had a very comical way about himself, but he would be the messenger of some ridiculous demands. One day I was preparing some of the documentation to mail out for the public trading packets, and Ed came with another outrageous demand. I politely smiled, stood up, got my purse and said, "Ed, stop doing his dirty work. So, you can now go and tell Cecil that I have withdrawn my two-week notice, and am now giving you a two-minute verbal notice. I quit, effective immediately."

Ed tried to stop me, other staff tried to stop me. I took my file and went home. That Friday was payday. I drove back to the office to get my check, which I was expecting to be in the amount of approximately $1300, and my check was for $436.00. Cecil had deducted every PTO day from the calendar year, stating in a letter with the check that I was not entitled to those days because I didn't stay for the entire year. I was enraged. I went into his office, and I cussed him up, down and sideways. He was such a mean and callous person. I went to my car looking for a knife because I swear I was going to slash his tires on his damn Saturn! Ed and the drivers tried to calm me down, I tried to go back into his office and slap him. I didn't. While I was angry, one of my bosses, Mike came in. He took me into his office and asked me what had gone on. I told him, then I told him about my file and that I was going to sue for harassment. Mike went into his pocket and gave me $1800 in cash and told me that they would not refuse my application for unemployment even though I had quit.

When God Opens Doors

I was able to spend time with my kids, and rest, recoup and decide what direction to go in next. I started researching colleges. The Community Colleges had good Nursing Programs, I would need to complete some pre-requisites, but I had some transferable credits from California. I had heard about a private Nursing school, so I called, St. Vincent's School of Nursing. I spoke with an admissions counselor by phone, and she informed me that they were currently testing for entry. She said that my credits should transfer; their program allows students to complete the additional courses most colleges require beforehand during their nursing program. They were in partnership with St. John's University. It would be more difficult and time consuming she told me. But, with hard work I could be a Registered Nurse in 2 years! I was excited. They had an entry exam, and the outcome determined who would be offered a spot in their 1998 Graduating Class, scheduled to begin in September of 1996. I scheduled the exam. I rushed to get started at ordering my transcripts and gathering all the needed documentation.

Two weeks later, I took the entry exam. Two weeks later I meet with an Admissions Specialist who advised me that I scored in the top 2% of applicants, guaranteeing me a seat in the class. I met with a financial advisor, and with grants and loans I would be covered, even having some extra money to help with expenses!

I was going to be a Nurse. I had told my Dad that before he died, he said I will be a good nurse, and I was on my way.

I needed to get childcare for Shayna and afterschool care for Marcel. I would be starting school in less than a month, and we couldn't afford to pay anyone if I was not working. I was told that there was a program to help low income Mothers with Daycare. I had applied before, but was told there was an 18-

month waiting list. I decided to try again; I stood in line at 6:30 in the morning and waited. I finally sat down with a worker and gave her my paperwork. She looked everything over, and told me I was approved, with a co-payment of $25.00 a week. I asked her what number I was on the waiting list, and she told me that the preschool was accepting enrollment, and if they accepted me, Shayna could start immediately. I went to the Pre-school and they enrolled Shayna and she would start that next Monday! Now, 3 months earlier, I was told there was an 18-month waiting list and now, I get approved and she has a spot. Not only that, but the co-payment covered both Shayna and Marcel, so I could find someone to keep him afterschool and the program would pay them also. When God opens doors, nobody, not anybody can close them but you.

Grindin'

Nursing school was not difficult for me. Thankfully, I have been blessed with good retention skills, good test taking skills, and great critical thinking skills. I found that study groups distracted me. I was better off studying on my own. I would simply go to class, take good notes, rewrite my notes at home and read my chapters. The most difficult section was Electrolytes, but once I got the hang of that, I was good. I carried at 3.47 GPA, I was Senior Class Vice-President and I enjoyed the Clinical Rotations where we watched and learned by doing in a hospital setting.

Our instructors were firm, and had high expectations. If your uniform was wrinkled, they sent you home. If you didn't have your equipment, you went home. If you missed more than two days of Clinicals, you may as well withdraw and try again next year. It was a small Catholic Nursing School with Old School Values, and I liked it. I excelled. Home life was difficult. Care of the house was entirely on me. K would take care of the yard and the outside, and I the inside. We were struggling financially. Still not seeing any benefits or income from the studio. The studio did get upgrades, however. K installed a private phone line in the basement. This made no sense to me; he said it was for business. I would soon learn that it was for business and pleasure, he and Marcus' pleasure with other women.

Cynthia and I were close. Both or families were struggling financially. We would figure things out, though. If she a chicken, I had some rice and some vegetables. If she made a cake, I bought the ice cream. We babysat for each other, and we comforted each other. She had difficulties with her in-laws, and I had difficulties with my in-laws. And my in-laws were her family, so she understood what I was going through. Our kids spent holidays together, and special occasions together. Cynthia taught me hospitality. She taught me how to serve a guest, and how to be observant of others. Growing up, we didn't ever have guests in our home. I became more domesticated around Cynthia. She taught me to bake and to cook. She was such a treasure to me during those times. She is one of the "just enough" that God gave me to get me through those difficult times.

Cynthia has Alissa who is close to age with Marcel, and Aaron who is close in age to Shayna. Our families spent a lot of time together. Anthony is Cynthia's husband; he is just an all-around good dude. His family is his priority. Seeing the difference between his headship of the home and K's confused me. I saw that K had the ability to be a great husband, father and friend. It just wasn't happening. The play stopped. The poems and romance stopped. He stopped really looking at me; I missed him, even when he was in the room with me. He seemed to have smiles and playful banter with everyone but me. I was attention deprived, but somehow, we always maintained a good sexual relationship. I was in for the long haul, though. I was still so in love with him. I craved him. I longed to be his partner, his friend, his woman, and his ride or die.

I began to suspect Kenny of cheating. I just felt it. Late phone calls, text messages on his SkyPager, women's voices on his answering machine all added up to cheating. There had been multiple signs that he was spending time elsewhere. The main sign being our continuing financial strain, even though, according to him, he was "In the Studio" or "At a Show" or "DJ'ing at a club." All that work and no money brought into the household was upsetting. There was some evidence of his earnings visible in the Basement Studio. But, I was kept in the dark about how much was being spent, and how much he was

making. I continued to try to focus on school and my kids.

I read his SkyPager one day and there were messages for

several females. One in particular, I called. She informed me

that she and Kenny were seeing each other. When I told her "We

have two kids." She responded, "He told me he has a daughter

with you, but that your son isn't his." This was very hurtful.

Here he was acting like my son's Father, telling people he was

his, and wanting me to arrange for his adoption, all the while not

claiming my son if it helped him to get with a female.

We argued and fought about the messages, and the female for

hours. At one point, V and Kim were trying to calm us. Kenny

was in the basement, and I was upstairs upset. I could hear his

basement phone ringing, so I took an extra phone and plugged it

into a jack that was in the kitchen. This jack was connected to

the basement phone line, and I heard Kenny talking with the

female that I had spoken to. I was pissed. Here I was, his

woman. And instead of trying to talk and reason with me, here

he was talking and reasoning with her. Kenny came upstairs and we argued some more. Eventually taking our argument upstairs into our bedroom. At one point we wrestled, and pushed each other and Kenny's anger built. He tried to pull me down the stairs by my hair, and I was trying to fight back. I was so hurt and angry. Kim and V witness our fight and separated us. I didn't consider it abuse, I looked at is as a fight. There would several similar incidents. I began to lose count. I would be at the mall or the grocery store and feel other females staring or commenting. People knew who I was, but I didn't know anything about them. This was alarming. I tried to talk to his parents, but they would only brush me off. They supported their son in everything he did, right or wrong. There were times when I would second-guess even what I saw with my own two eyes.

Snakes in My Grass

Kenny started a company *"FINGERS Ent."* A young neighbor girl began to come around, and I was told she could sing. And into our lives enters: J. She was about 16 years old, and she lived a few houses down on the block that intersected ours. She was from a bi-racial family of four girls, her father was white and her mother was some type of West Indian. I didn't like the situation from the start. She really could sing, but it just didn't sit well with me. They would be in the basement for hours and hours, singing lyrics that we in no way suitable for a teenager. I would over hear conversations about sex; she would call K all hours of the day and night, eventually even calling when we were away on vacation. I expressed my concerns to K to be met with "You're just jealous." Ronique and I were both concerned. I thought that she and Marcus were having some sort of twisted fling. This would continue for about a year. And I tolerated it. I was busy with school, and the kids. She babysat a time or two when K finally would take me to dinner or a movie.

I began to wonder if K and J had something going on. She just seemed attached to him." J invited me to one of the school musicals she was in. I went and this was when I really got to meet her family. Things still didn't feel right, but I was giving it all a chance to see if I was over-reacting. I was actually in the studio once with K, when she knocked on the door and came down the stairs, she was going to a High-School dance or something, and she came to show K how she looked. He told her to turn around so he could see and she spun around. And I could have slapped the shit out of him. It was just so wrong. I knew then that things weren't right. But, let him tell it, "You are just jealous." I began to play detective at that point. I would go into the basement, which was locked, but that never stopped a woman, I would look through the computer, look through the locked office, listen to their answering machine messages. In one message, J blew a kiss at the end. Then when I brought up the contact list on the computer, J's number was listed with the code of 69. That was just plain crazy. One day, I needed a ride from school. Anthony gave me a ride, and when we were coming down the hill and approaching J's house I see K in the Red truck Kenny's big Brother had left him when he died, and J's head in in the driver's side window. It looked like they were kissing. Anthony pulled the car around them, and they saw us drive past. They pretended to just be talking, and even Anthony made excuses.

Everyone I talked to about it told me I was crazy and that K was not that stupid. We argued and fought that night. On another occasion, K's parents were in town visiting once and I started to notice that K was leaving earlier and earlier for work. He used to leave at 6am. And now he is leaving at 5? One morning I got up and followed him. He went straight to J's house. One night, he got in his truck and left my house and parked at hers, going in the opposite way. I walked over to the house, and there were keys in the door hanging. I knocked and rang the doorbell, and no one answered. Then finally, her Dad came to the door and I asked for Kenny. Kenny comes out of a back room, and goes off on me. I talked with his Mother about it, and although she did admit it was strange, *she* tried to convince me that Kenny wouldn't make such a huge mistake.

I began to go back to church. I have always prayed, and read books based on Bible teachings, but hadn't really been a regular member at a church. I didn't take the kids at first, because I was visiting new churches and I wanted time to focus and see what they were about. Another reason was that I just needed a break to breathe. I needed some time alone. I needed some time for me. I found a church on the other side of Staten Island by the mall, it was small, the teachings were good, and it was Spirit Filled. I went most Sundays, crying my eyes out, searching for God, searching for strength, soaking up the spirit. I would pray at home all the time. I knew that I was to anoint my house, and pray, read my Bible and teach the kids. I would start and stop. Rise up, and fall. Those were some of the most trying times of my life. I felt so betrayed, and I attributed to the fact that we were living in sin. I was fornicating and that's why our lives had been infiltrated by the enemy.

"What the hell?" I examined the folded paper I pulled out of the door pocket of our car. It had J's name on it. As I read it my heart pounded hard in my chest. It was a doctor's visit receipt, and a folded prescription for birth control pills. My mind was bombarded with pictures of Kenny taking this young girl to the doctor to get birth control pills! When I confronted Kenny, he was his usual evasive self. Told me, *"She just needed a ride from school. I didn't take her to no damn doctor. That*

doesn't even make sense." Questioning Kenny turned into nagging, and even I was tired of my nagging. I didn't know what to do. I had two kids, I was thousands of miles away from my family, I didn't have any extra money, and I was in Nursing School. I wanted desperately to finish Nursing School. I prayed hard to keep from losing my mind. It felt like I was in the Twilight Zone. I fought against depression and anxiety, but they took hold of me anyway.

Fingers ENT had been hired to have an outside performance at the opening of a neighborhood clinic. J and her friends practiced at our house, and even with all the signs, it just didn't make sense to me that Kenny would be so stupid. I was in a battle with myself, wanting to believe he was not capable of being so low down. When the day of the performance came, I was helping, and we were all running around preparing things. I can't remember how, but somehow, I ended up driving J to the site where the performance would take place. Things had continued to prove to me that something inappropriate was happening, and so I asked her. *"J, I need to know, are you fucking*

159

with Kenny?" She put on a show, telling me *"No, never. He's like*

a brother to me. I would never disrespect you like that." I still

didn't know what to believe, but I didn't believe either of them.

Me in 1997, in our home in Staten Island.

Christmas came Kenny and I argued about J. We argued almost daily. Even worse, if we weren't arguing we weren't talking at all. Every approach I tried was not working. The only thing I had any control over in our house was myself.

Valentine's Day 1997, Fingers ENT had a show at a local restaurant just a few blocks from my house. Everyone was busy transporting equipment, preparing the stage, and running around. K had partnered, against my better judgment with Mus and Noel; Noel was my friend Monique's, sister. They had partnered with equal interest, when K had bought most of the equipment, and K and I were paying all of the house bills. It just didn't make sense to me why he would give people a vested interest that had not contributed equally into the business.

Kenny started doing something that was very strange. He made the back of his Nissan Mini-truck into a bed. *A Real Bed.* He put pillows and blankets, and I stood and watched him one day. *"What the hell do you need a bed in the truck for?"* I never got an answer.

I went upstairs to change and found a card, it was a basic Valentine's Day Card. Had bears or something on it, it was cute, but not romantic. He also gave me a small box of candy. I changed clothes and went out to the driveway to get in my car and Mus was blocking me. I yelled downstairs for him to come and move the car and he didn't come. I walked down further into the basement to find him, because I didn't want to be late. When I saw a box of candy, just like mine, and a card sitting in a chair. It had been opened. I picked up the card and read it. My hurt and anger swelled up inside of me. I was devastated. The Card was romantic, and it talked about love, and I love you because of this, and I love you because of that. That was a card that I deserved, and here he had given it to J. It had her name on it, and his usual K at the bottom. I became irate, I yelled for Mus, who came out of nowhere and I told him to move his car. I had told him one hundred times before to not park in my driveway. I think that is so disrespectful, don't park in a driveway where you don't pay bills. He tried to calm me down; he didn't know what was wrong with me. He finally moved his car and I drove to where the show was to take place.

I walked in and I stood near a wall and just waited. I didn't say anything to anybody. I wear my emotions on my face, so I am sure I was visibly upset. Cynthia and Anthony were there, as was K, J, another female, I forget her name because she was a non-factor, but she was a friend of Noel's that was supposed to be helping in a managerial sense in Noel's absence. I stood against the wall and waited. J decided to come near me and put on a concerned face and ask me, *"What's wrong?"* as if she were a friend. I kept my cool and told her, *"If I were you, I would get out of my face, right now."* She looked confused and continued to ask me what's wrong, and I began to cuss her out. I called her a lying hoe, asking her how could she babysit my kids and be fucking my man, I told her that she better not come to my home anymore. Somehow, we wound up in the bathroom, where she continued to deny it all. I yelled and screamed. And then I was put out of the restaurant.

The next morning, I drove to J's house. It was a Friday. I rang the doorbell and her Dad answered, I asked to speak to him and to her Mother. Her Mother came to the door, I showed them the card, and told them to keep their daughter away from my home. Her Mother was rude and didn't seem to care, *"It's my Sabbath."* Was all she would say. *"Well, you allow your daughter to come to my home and disrespect me on your Sabbath."* Was my response. I told her parents to keep her from my house and I threatened to beat her ass if I saw her there again. J showed up in the doorway shouting, *"Did you tell my Mom you called me a Bitch?"* I responded, *"You are a Bitch, for disrespecting me and my kids in my home."* I was amazed that they did not seem surprised or angered at being told their daughter was involved with Kenny. I do regret having my kids in the car to observe what took place. I should never have taken them there. I was out of control with anger, depression and anxiety. All I knew to do was fight, and I felt like I was in the fight of my life.

My house began to feel like a cage. I was trapped. I had no control over who came and went and I was mentally exhausted from all of it. Anxiety built. I felt like I was a fool, and everyone else was laughing at me. But, I refused to break. I began to sleep whenever I could, which eventually was more than I should. I hated that house, I hated that I had no control over what and who my kids were being exposed to, I hated that I had no idea of how to change my life, and I hated that Kenny didn't seem to care.

Can it get any worse?

I was unhappy, and I was tired of being broke. I also felt that I needed to be out of the house more to force Kenny into participating in raising the kids. As long as I was at home, the responsibility fell upon me. So, I started working for Bryson Insurance Agency. Bryson's owner was a young, black man from Staten Island, names Thomas. It was a busy place, and most young, black people had their insurance policies through Bryson. Tom's friends would hang there, and he partook of many business ventures. There was a T-shirt printing business and clothing line, the travel agency Kenny's big Brother has been a partner in was still up and operating, and they even stepped into the music arena with a studio and management company. Cynthia worked there and got me hired. He would pay me cash under the table and it helped. I meet a lot of the community working here, and it kept me busy. And busy was good; when I was busy my mind was off of my troubles. I would be in school four to five days out of the week, and I would work at Bryson for anywhere from three to eight hours a day. When Kenny had to he would step up and be a good father, but, if I was around the parenting fell to me. It was exhausting.

I had fell out with Mus and Noel after the Valentine's Day Incident. They did not respect my home. They did not respect me. They did not respect my children. They were only concerned about music and becoming famous. I felt like I was drowning. I didn't bite my tongue, I told all of them what I thought of them and their outright disrespect for my home. K even went so far as to tell me that J would come to my home, and

I had no say so over it. And I responded, *"And she will get her ass kicked."* and that was that. Her older sisters and her Momma complained to Kenny that I was "Crazy". They were supporting 16-year-old J fucking a 25-year-old Father of 2, in the home he shared with me. *"And I am the crazy one?"*

The whole situation was crazy, Noel was sexing with Mus, Kenny was sexing with J. Actually, I was thinking they were just a freaky group sexing each other. Not one of them having any respect for me, my children, or my home.

Kenny was slick, or so he thought. I discovered a little scheme he had arranged with our Postman. As I sat on the Sun-porch looking out the window I saw the mailman walk up the steps to our porch, and back down the steps. A few minutes later I checked the porch. *"Hmmmm, no mail in the mailbox, and no large boxes on the porch. Why would he take the time to walk up the steps, but, not leave any mail?"* Something told me to look under the mat. And sure enough, Kenny's mail was under the mat. One night I dreamed that there was something in his safe in the studio's office I needed to see. Kenny was not home, so I went down to the basement, opened the doors he thought I couldn't open, opened the safe he thought I could not open, and inside was K's credit card bill with a hotel charge on it, it was a hotel right across the bridge in Jersey. Of course, I would confront him. But, it didn't seem to matter. He was living the life of a single man, and my questions only seemed to irritate him.

They Will Dream Dreams

S, pregnant with K's baby. Somebody he says he knew from school. He denied having a relationship, denied loving her, denied wanting the baby. I cried, I was an indescribable mess. Kenny cried, too, and he promised me that he loved me. He promised me that he would do whatever it takes to keep his family. He made a million promises that night. All I could think about was how stupid I felt, and how stupid I looked to everyone around me. It made me wonder if I was wrong about J. *"I mean, how can he possibly find the time for two women?"* I started to second-guess myself. The situation had me questioning my sanity. Nothing made any sense.

I decided to write S, the girl who was pregnant with K's baby a letter, in the letter I explained that I was not going anywhere. I explained that I was not giving up school for anybody, and that Kenny was going to continue taking care of us until I was done. Not that he was doing a great job, but it was more than I could do on my own. I also explained that I very well might stay with him. The only one who would decide and control that would be me. She didn't respond. But, she did complain to my boss, so I know she got the letter. After some investigating, I found out that she drove a white Honda. Then it all fell together. Kenny had a white Honda two-door Accord in my driveway installing a radio a few months prior. He had driven the car over, and told me it belonged to a co-worker. He was such an arrogant asshole. Once I knew her address, I knew I had seen his truck parked near her apartments on several occasions.

I had several dreams about K back then. I would wake up and have names of women, and research would prove me right. I became embarrassed to be seen in Staten Island. Everywhere I went it felt like people were looking at me, knowing that Kenny was screwing with one of their friends, cousins or daughters. So many people knew me, where I lived, what I looked like, and what l drove that I felt vulnerable. I was in strange territory, trying to make it home and he was making me feel more and more like a stranger in a strange land every day. I remember being at the mall, and a young woman complimenting me on Shayna and Marcel, and then hearing her tell her friend that she was dating Kenny. It was becoming too much to bear. School became more difficult, but I still managed to keep my grades up. I prayed a lot. Asking God for clarity, and for sanity. There were many days that I would have fought or argued, but instead I just went to sleep. Looking back, I believe it was the Holy Spirit calming me and comforting me and keeping me from losing it. When his family would visit, giving Kenny's sister a reason to come over even though she knew I did not like her, they would notice me sleeping a lot and would make comments and talk about me to Kenny. They noticed my sleeping, but they never said anything to Kenny about his behavior. When they were there, my stress level was so elevated. I know there were days the Holy Spirit put me to sleep instead of allowing me to lose my cool. I tried talking to his parents about what I was going through, they just defended their son. I once asked his Father how he would feel if I were his daughter. He couldn't put the shoe on the other foot, he wanted his son to have the pretty picture, and no matter how ugly the scene behind closed doors.

Friends and Acquaintances

Kenny's sister became engaged. Her fiancé was Cynthia's husband's cousin. So, it was like a big family thing. The families all knew each other well, and everyone was excited. I have never been one to stay mad or hold a grudge, and Kenny's sister seemed to be making an effort to be friendly around this time. So, when she asked me to be a bridesmaid in her wedding and for Shayna to be a flower girl, I obliged. I began to help her make plans, visiting dress shops, shopping with her, planning what the bridal party would wear and even helping to coordinate the wedding. I enjoyed it, I believe that every woman deserves a beautiful wedding and I was helping her based simply on the fact that she was family. No matter what our pasts had been, I would help her have a beautiful wedding.

Being a part of her bridal party put me in close contact with her friends. As we began to spend more time together, her friends and her in-laws began to warm up to me and me to them. We all got along well. I had to work closely with her friends and in-laws to plan the Bridal Shower.   It was a beautiful wedding, and a few months after, it was time to plan the Baby Shower for her second child. I worked with her friends to plan that also. I was ready to get over our pasts and forgive. And I did. We were all able to celebrate Kenny's sister's Birthday together, and things between us seemed to be going well. I began to relax around her; I thought that she was finally going to act like she was my family.

The Bridal Party for Kenny's sister's

Changes On The Outside & The Inside

I began to lose weight by walking and changing my eating habits. Between school, work and the kids, I barely had time to eat. I began walking our Rottweiler, Nitro, in the evenings to reduce my stress and to have a break from the house and kids. Inside, I felt uneasy about everything. I knew that I absolutely had to finish school. There were no options. As far as my family, I did not know what the future held and that made me very uneasy. For the first time in my life, I experienced rejection. And I did not know how to accept it, so I did the only thing I knew how to do, and that was to fight it.

Me at a backyard bar-b-que during those months of weight loss.

I felt like Kenny had a hundred reasons to respect me, a thousand reasons to like me, and a million reasons to love me. So, my mind just could not grasp that he did not want all of the things we had talked about sharing. I had risked so much, and I was not willing to release my hopes and dreams. We would follow the plan, no matter what obstacles appeared in our path. I felt like we could get over them. In the background of our lives was the pain caused by Kenny's infidelity. There was a woman carrying his child, and that thought never left. We didn't really talk about it. I wondered if he was visiting her, being there for her the way he was there for me when I was expecting Shayna.

Stress began to eat away at me, and it showed in my face. I was getting thinner and thinner. Being busty and thick in the rear, I had always carried a little extra weight. But, that time, my face began to thin, and my checks and eyes began to hallow. I did enjoy being a size six. Kenny was attempting to be more attentive at the time, so when I planned to go to a comedy club in Jersey with my friends Kenny went shopping with me, and bought my outfit.

Cynthia, Ronique and I drove in my 280Z from Staten Island to A's house in Jersey where Angie and Lisa were waiting for us. We drank a little and headed over to Rascal's Comedy Club where A worked in the office. I needed a night out. My girls knew the pain I was in, and it felt good to laugh and smile for a change. We had excellent seats at a table directly in front of the stage. We had plenty to drink by the time the headlining comedian came out. He was hilarious. The entire audience was cracking up when one of my girls became sick from all the alcohol. She was sitting next to me. The club was packed, and the lights were low as the comedienne entertained us all. *"Rayna, come with me to the bathroom. I'm going to be sick."* She whispered to me. *"Girl, we can't get up. He is going to clown us!"* I told her. Everyone knew you do not walk out or in during a comedy show, or you become the comedy. *"Please, I don't feel good."* She leaned over and held my left wrist. *"I'm gonna throw up!"* She tried to whisper, but it was way louder than a whisper. I stood up and helped her to get to her feet and we walked to the bathroom as I held her up to keep her from stumbling into a fall.

She vomited as soon as we got into the bathroom. I got a wet towel to wash her face and one for the back of her neck. She sat on the floor, near the toilet. She was loaded, and so was the toilet. I was missing the show, but couldn't leave my girl. I stayed with her, waiting to see if the vomiting helped her to feel better. After ten or fifteen minutes, my other girl came in to check on us. We switched places, so I could hear some of the comedy show. As I tried to sneak back to my seat, the comedienne drew attention to me, *"Awww, look-a-here. That's what I'm talking about. I love a thick woman, look at her, that's just how I like them."* The light was directed to me and I smiled and stood for a moment before sitting down. I laughed at the attention, and was just relieved it was a good comment that he made. I looked up at him as he stood over our table telling his jokes. *"Now, LA women, they are a trip."* And he went on to comment about women from LA, and I had to interject. He smiled and stood with his attention on me for a moment as he teased that I was objecting to his joke. The audience laughed with me, and the show continued. When the show ended, I was approached by his manager who asked if I would go backstage to meet him. *"Sure, but, I have to check on my friend first."* I replied. He told me to come to the stairwell when I was done and I would be taken to him.

Our girl was still sick from the alcohol. We stood in the bathroom and talked for a while, trying to see if she were okay to get up and leave the club. I whispered to Ronique that I wanted her to come with me, and we left and went to the stairwell. We were taken upstairs to the dressing room, and formally introduced. He was very attractive, and I was intrigued by the fact that he noticed me. Ronique and I sat with him and the other comedienne's and talked and laughed. As I got up to excuse myself, he pulled me to the side and asked me if I would meet up with him at his hotel. *"I have to get my girls home, but if you are still up when I am done I will think about it."* I flirted back. We exchanged numbers and Ronique and I went to look for our friends. None of which realized that I had been in the dressing room.

We drove back to A's house, and then I drove Cynthia and Ronique back to Staten Island. After dropping Cynthia off, Ronique and I sat in front of her high-rise and talked about the evening. My phone rang as we talked, and it was him. I convinced Ronique to come with me, so I would not do anything that I would regret.

We drove to the Hotel, and the valet parked my car. I was excited to be having such an exciting night. Everything I had been dealing with was far away, and it was the first time in a long time that I felt wanted again. We sat in the room and talked for several hours. When we got up to leave, Ronique walked out the door and he pulled me to him and hugged me. My hand went into his robe and rubbed across his stomach and held onto his side. I was glad Ronique had come along, because just the touch of his finely defined body made me not want to leave. He kissed me on the cheek and I left. I drove Ronique home, and we laughed and talked about the good and the bad of all that was going on in my life.

The next morning, Kenny was up bright and early and began to dress for church. He told me that he was going to church with Mus. *"That's some bullshit."* I thought to myself. But I didn't argue. Kenny never went to church, but I had other things on my mind anyway. When Kenny left, I called my new friend. He was glad to hear from me, and asked me to come back to the Hotel. I got up, put on a cute little summer dress and some wedges, got the kids ready and loaded them up in the car. Ronique was waiting in the lobby when I pulled up to drop the kids off.

He opened the door. His shirt was off and his six-pack was a welcome relief from my troubles. I walked in and sat down. He had ordered breakfast, and we talked as he ate. I had no appetite for food. He talked about his Television show, and made a few calls. He spoke to my very favorite female singer of all time, and I hid my excitement. After his calls, he asked me to lie down with him. He had another show that night, and said he needed rest.

I laid down next to him on the king size bed. He rested. And I lay there taking in my surroundings. I woke up to his hands pulling me into him. He undressed me, and we had sex. It was sweet relief. I felt beautiful. And I felt something I hadn't felt in a long time, *wanted*. His body was perfect, and as I explored it I felt a release. He was just what I needed, right when I needed it. I showered, dressed and left with a list of his phone numbers for his various residences in my purse. I didn't plan on using them, but it felt good to have them.

I enjoyed my secret; I felt avenged, in a way. I had been cheated on and lied to for years. Kenny had a child on the way, and I had to live with it. *"I'm not saying it was right, but it didn't feel very wrong."*

Players Will Pay

I was home early one afternoon when the mail arrived. There was a letter addressed to me with no return address. I opened it and in side was a white sheet of paper with the words, "FINGERS you are cut off." Inside was a latex glove with the fingers cut off. The next day another letter arrived that stated Kennith was spreading Genital Warts. Because Kenny's sister seemed to be concerned about me, and had me thinking that she was sympathetic to me, I confided in her about the letter and told her that I thought they were from S, pregnant with K's baby. I told Kenny about the letters after that and rushed to the Doctor and was cleared of having HPV, the virus that causes Genital Warts.

Within the week, another envelope arrived. This one contained a type written letter. It threatened that Kenny would lose "your job, your house and your kids." I took this letter very personally. *"Why were people speaking of my children?"* They were innocent. My kids did not deserve to have their lives upturned because the adults around them were doing wrong. The letter also was proof that the letters were coming from J, and not from S, pregnant with K's baby. The letter told me that J and Kenny had been sexually involved. Everything was exploding in Kenny's face, and he knew it. The pregnancy had taken the focus off of J and onto his cheating with S, pregnant with K's baby. These letters told me that he was screwing all of us. J was retaliating for being barred from my home, and now she was even angrier because another woman was pregnant. Everything around me was on fire, and the flames were illuminating Kennith and his wrongs. Everything was coming into the light. As he grew weaker from the stress, I grew stronger. I refused to crumble, and my God wouldn't let me.

The letter accused Kenny of committing statutory rape, and it ended with a demand for the Master Copies of *"any song or work that J recorded in FINGERS studio."* I hated that I was right! Down the street there was a now nineteen-year-old girl that had been in my home, babysat my kids, joined us for holiday dinners and was now accusing Kenny of RAPE! A few blocks away was a female accusing Kenny of fathering her unborn child. All of my intuition and my fears were reality. All I could do was pray. And perfectly timed, as everything Kenny was doing was falling right into my lap, when Kenny's phone rang that night while he was in the shower. The events of the day made me bold and I answered the phone. It was a female. I questioned her, and she told it all. She and her cousin were the reason for that Sunday "Church" Service that Kenny and Marcus had a few weeks earlier. She told me that she and Kenny had sex "once". And she told me that Kenny told her he "had a crazy Baby's Momma." And that he was "single and lived with his roommate, Mus." And she believed him because she always called the "home phone." I informed her that the phone she called was in my basement, and that Mus had lived there rent-free for several months. By then, Kenny was out of the shower and I gave him the phone. He denied ever sleeping with her, and told her that she knew full well that he had a woman and a family. *"He has time for woman after woman, but there are times I am lonely."* I couldn't understand why.

I shut our house down, and this time Kenny agreed. Mus and Noel would no longer have access to my home. I was fed up, and Kenny knew it. He changed the locks and told them that the studio was shut down. All the while, I continued with my Nursing courses and Clinical rotations at the hospital. I continued to keep a 3.75 GPA, and I continued to Mother my children. No matter what was going on at home, I could not risk messing up my education, and I would not risk my kids suffering needlessly. It was only by God's grace that I was able to function. And it was only by God's grace that Kenny had me on his team!

Two days after shutting the studio down, I answered the telephone at home and a man who identified himself as a NYC Detective asked for Kennith Moorer. Kenny got on the phone, and I could hear the nervousness in his voice. He waved at me to run upstairs and pick up the other line and listen. The Detective was explaining that J had gone to the station and reported that

Kennith had committed Statutory Rape against her. The words echoed in my head, but at that point, not much surprised me. The Detective said that Marcus was with J when she made the repot and that he had given a statement acknowledging it to be true and that Marcus was the key witness. Kenny was requested to come to the Police Station the next morning to meet with the Detectives assigned to the case. The Detective went on to say that he could have come to our home and arrested Kenny at that moment, but he didn't want to have the me or the children involved in this matter and that at that point a warrant had not yet been issued. Kenny hung up the phone, and his fear was evident. He called his parents and his sister, and we called Cynthia and Anthony.

I was angry at everybody. This was exactly what I was afraid of. And everyone had told me I was wrong. Well, apparently Kenny was *"that stupid."* Everyone had made me out to be insecure and crazy, when what I had accused Kenny of did not even compare to what was really going on. Kenny was spending time everywhere but at home with his kids and I, and now it would be the kids and I who would pay for his mistakes.

I was so sad that I was right. I wanted to be wrong. I had just enough energy to protect my children and make sure my grades did not suffer. I knew the truth, and I knew what I was facing. As much as the truth hurt, the truth allowed me to focus. Knowing what I was up against was better than speculation. I prayed for peace. I prayed that I would be strong enough to survive what we were facing. The humiliation was heavy, and the heartache was costly. I could not look left, or right, I had to keep my focus to the future because the present was unbearable. I refused to break, and I refused to allow anyone to hurt my children. All I could do was pray, and I prayed long and hard. I prayed and I prayed, I prayed all night and my prayer language came forth for the first time. I didn't know what to pray for, but the Holy Spirit did.

Compassion

I felt sorry, and scared, for Kenny. I have always had a soft heart. Even if I wanted to just throw my hands up and leave I couldn't. I had to ride this out because Nursing School failure was NOT an option. I had to ride it out because my kid's stability was the most important goal in my life. And I had to ride it out simply because I loved Kennith. No matter what he did, no matter the pain he caused, no matter the heartache, I simply loved that man. And when I looked at him, I felt sorry for him. My heart ached because of him, in spite of him, and for him. I would not leave him when he was down.

I was forced to think about my own mistakes. I had once been sixteen and in a relationship with a twenty-five-year-old man. He, too, had a girlfriend. I was reaping what I had sown. My wrongs were similar, but not the same. I knew the decisions I made at sixteen to lay up with a grown man were my decision; and I never would have accused him of rape. I was making grown up decisions, and paid a grown-up price. I never hated her. It astonished me that a teenager could be so cunning and devious. I felt sorry for J, and I wondered if she would be able to stand when it came her time to reap. She had been in my home, ate my food, babysat my children, helped Kenny pick out my Christmas gifts. That was weird.

The next morning, we had an appointment with Duane Felton. We sat in his office as he questioned Kenny, researched the accusations, and made contact with the Detectives. A warrant was issued, and the Detectives were told that Kennith would be turning himself in. Kenny paid the retainer with borrowed money, and Mr. Felton drove him to the Precinct.

My mind was spinning. Kenny needed to make it to work not only for his paycheck, but to keep the kid's health insurance and benefits in effect. At home, I made calls to Kenny's good friend, Giz. The news of Kenny's arrest was already spreading among our friends and associates. Giz said he would help me to get some of the funds needed by selling Kenny's studio equipment. We would know the next morning if we would need Bail money. It was hard to sleep. I hugged my daughter as she slept, and I prayed that God would protect my children.

I had been in court before for M. Never in a million years would I have thought I would be in court for Kennith. I listened to the cases that came before his. I wondered how many people in the room would know Kennith. When Kennith's case came before the Judge, the Lawyers spoke and the Judge agreed to release Kenny on his own recognizance. He would be released that day, and I was glad that I didn't have to gather up bail money. Mr. Felton met with me and told me that he would get Kenny and bring him home.

Kenny told me that the US Postal Police came to the jail to see him. He was suspended without pay. J's Father had a friend who was a Postal Police Officer, and he told Kenny they would be investigating J's allegations that they had sex several times in the Postal Truck! I could only shake my head. Cynthia, Monique, Ronique, and Kim were my confidants. So much was coming out that I got tired of talking about it. They all knew what my family was going through, and they were all there for me as much as they could be.

"How are my kids going to eat? How are we going to pay our rent? " I never once felt that Kenny was right, but I did not feel that my kids should be targeted to such an extent. And J was not innocent. I had asked her myself. She had babysat my kids! They were both at fault. S, pregnant with K's baby knew Kenny had kids, she knew we lived together. Yes, Kenny was to blame, but everyone shared some blame, everyone including ME!

A's husband had an import and export business, and Kenny and V went to work for him. He was paying Kenny ten dollars an hour under the table, and I still had my job at Bryson. I knew how to stretch a dollar, and Kenny was able to borrow from his parents, and from Kenny's sister. Times were tough. I began to compartmentalize my emotions. I couldn't break. I had to keep going. I pushed myself to continue in school. I was nominated for Class President. No one at school would probably ever think I was going through what I was at home. Church was my refuge. I was still attending the small, spirit-filled church on the other side of Staten Island. I would shed all my tears and all my fears and all my pain at the altar. Sometimes, I wondered what the other church members thought of my tears and my being on the altar every single Sunday. But then I realized, just as I looked okay on the outside and was in the fight of my life on the inside, *"they might be fighting on the inside, too."*

Enemies and So-Called Friends and Business Partners

"You are served." The documents said that Marcus and Noel were suing Kenny for the business, for the equipment, for Master Copies and for being locked out of our home. *"How the hell can you sue me because I locked you out of my house?"* All I could think of was the blatant disregard for my kids. People who you fed, housed, provided utilities for, spent holidays with, and loved were attacking from all sides. *"And, YES Kennith was wrong! But, why were they so hungry to take steps that were not only hurting him, but hurting us?"*

It was coming at us from every direction. This meant an additional Fifteen-hundred-dollar retainer for Mr. Felton. Once again, we sat in his office as we dissected the details of the case. Kenny tried to keep his head up, and I knew with everything in me that the strength God had given me to get through this and to stand with him was what kept our family from imploding. I strategized, and planned, and helped navigate Kenny's defense. Facts and details came out that I knew nothing about. We dissected the contract that Kenny had signed giving Marcus and Noel an equal share of FINGERS, ENT when they had not put in an equal financial share or shared an equal part of the workload. They were claiming equipment Kenny had bought and was dumb enough to purchase not in his name, but in the name of FINGERS, ENT. Marcus had an American Express Card for the business, and I didn't even know the business had lines of credit. It was a mess.

Kennith's saving grace was that I felt my kids were being punished. If J, Marcus, and Noel had done it another way. If they had reached out to me, or apologized to me, or shown any type of concern for my family, Kenny may have been on his own. But, I was not going to just walk away and allow self-righteous people who were perfectly fine with my kids and I being hurt to steamroll over our livelihood.

Kennith's parents helped Kenny tremendously with money during those months. They arrived about a week after and stayed longer than a month. I was appreciative, and thankful. Kenny's sister and I were on speaking terms, and I was still thinking that she was finally understanding me and accepting me as family. I knew that I was doing everything I could to help Kenny and to protect my family. It seemed evident, and I thought that if his family never respected me before, they would definitely respect me after seeing me ride with him the way I was.

A and I began to get closer. She started spending more time with me, and with my kids. I was so thankful that Kenny at least had some type of income. It was not close to his Postal income, but it was so much better than nothing. As our Lawyer prepared Kenny's defense for the Rape Case, I told my story. The true story. I didn't hold back on how I had accused them of having sex, what I had seen and what I had heard. I told Mr. Felton about the night I overheard J in the studio talking about losing her virginity and her sex style and how I went off on

Kenny for having a young girl talking like that around adults. A was in the studio when the conversation took place. He interviewed A, and thought she would be a good witness to explain the details of that conversation.

The Grand Jury would be hearing the charges to decide if the State would pursue the charges that had been filed. Mr. Felton thought that I should testify. And that A should testify. He said that Kennith should NOT take the stand for the Grand Jury. The day came. Kennith's parents had gone home, and it seemed like all the worry and all the effort was on me. I never once heard them speak to Kenny about his actions, scold him, or even acknowledge the wrong that was done. They were defensive and protective of their son, though. They would not acknowledge that he had any fault. From their point of view, people were attacking Kenny unjustly.

Mr. Felton, Kenny, Angie and I sat in a room and waited to be called into the Grand Jury room. I was told to tell the truth. And I was told to find a way to read the letter threatening Kenny if he didn't turn over the Master Recordings. A was told to tell the truth about her interactions with J, what she witnessed when she was in the presence of Kennith and J, and the conversation they had discussing J's sexual history. Kennith was nervous. Mr. Felton told us that J and Mus had testified the day before. The Grand Jury heard the accusations, and Mr. Felton discussed their testimony and explained his legal approach to the case as we waited.

I walked in the room. Two lawyers sat at a table, and there were about 25 people sitting in chairs that elevated per row like a theater that watched me as I walked in and sat down. The judge was sitting at his desk with a gavel. I don't remember him having a robe on. I was told to state my name and swear to tell the truth and the questions began. They asked me about my home, my kids, and me and K's relationship. I did not lie. They asked me about J. I told them she frequented my home, the studio, babysat my kids, invited me to her school musical, and I told them about the day I questioned her in my car and her responses. They asked me about S, pregnant with K's baby and how I felt about her having K's child. I told them that I wasn't pleased, but decided to stay with Kennith. They asked me about genital warts, and did I know what they were and if Kenny had them. I told them I was a Nursing School Student, knew about Genital Warts and never saw any on Kenny. And I provided Doctor's notes for both of us in support of that fact. They asked me if I thought Kenny had raped J. I told them about the day I went to her home and asked her parents to keep her away from my home and the way her parents treated me. I also told them that she continued to come to my home, after that when I was not at home. I testified about the messages I saw and heard, and the way she called him even when we were away on vacation. Then they asked me again if I thought he had raped J. I then opened the letter and began to read. I was able to read the letter in its entirety.

I told them that I have three older sisters, and J has two. And I told them that if my sisters thought I had been raped, they would be at the man's house beating him down and not writing letters asking for Master Copies. I then talked about Marcus living in my basement, free, and my locking him out just prior to him giving his testimony to the police. I also told the Grand Jury that just a few weeks earlier, Kenny and I stood in church as Marcus' daughter was Christened and became her God-Parents. It seemed that the only thing that happened since the Christening was the closing of the studio. And I was excused from the courtroom.

Kenny and I at the Church for the Christening of our God Daughter.

I walked back to the room where Our Attorney, Kenny, A and I waited. We spoke to our Attorney a little longer and were then excused to go home. A decision would be made public tomorrow. We sat in our Attorney's Office as he told us the District Attorney would not be pressing charges and gave K paperwork stating it would be removed from his record. K's union coordinated his return to work and repayment of lost income.

I did not go to the Civil Case. Kenny would have to handle that on his own. All the secrets and lies of FINGERS, ENT would have to be unraveled without my help. The Civil Case ended; of course, they could not demand access to my home. They did not get much, if I remember correctly, they did not get the Master Copies, and Kenny had to give them some equipment and that was about it. Monique got married after that, and Kenny and I went. Noel being Monique's sister, I couldn't help but feel the tension. Monique was on my side, she understood me and what I had went through. She was the only one that ever spoke up for me. She called J and told her what she thought of her. Monique and I were never the same after that though. Our friendship was another casualty of that war. I resented Kenny for that, as I resented him for so many other things.

Will This Ever End?

I was spent. Mentally, Physically, Spiritually, Emotionally exhausted. After fighting so hard against all of the mistakes Kenny had brought into my life, it seemed like things would never be right. The court case and the Civil Suit had overshadowed the reality that Kenny could very well have gotten another woman pregnant. No matter how he protested, that baby was his. I dreamed it, and it wasn't the first time I had a prophetic dream. I had been having them since I was a child. It has always been in my nature to stand strong during life's trials and tribulations. With the wear and tear eventually showing when the troubles have faded into the memories, it is then that the damage appears. It is then that the fear shows up.

This time was no different. And so, I slept. And I slept. And I slept. Thus, beginning my love affair with sleep. I slept as often as I could, as long as I could. Which wasn't much with two small children, but it was enough for K's parents and sister to begin to make remarks about. They were back on an extended vacation. They would come and stay for weeks, even over a month at a time. I both enjoyed and dreaded their company.

After the fiasco, my family had just gone through, they actually

spoke to K about me sleeping all the time. No mention of what

he just put me through, no thanks for the strength I displayed

during his time of need. No praise for maintaining my kids, my

grades and my home during the toughest time of my life. And

Kenny didn't defend me. I overhead multiple conversations

while I was *"asleep"* in my room. I wondered why? They had

lived in the house for years and they knew just how voices

carried. And yet they would talk about me anyway. Never once

did I hear anyone chastise Kenny for the havoc he had wreaked

on his family. Let them tell it, he had done no wrong.

I continued to do well in Nursing School. Forcing

myself to perform my Motherly duties, and to continue to work.

I would take my walks with the dog in the evenings to relax.

And then I see that damn White Honda parked on a side street as

I walked. The street was a small one I went down every

weekday to pick Myles up from After School Care at his

Elementary. Everywhere I turned, I was slapped in the face by the fact that my man was a Dog. I didn't even bother to tell Kenny what I saw. I was so tired of the subject of everyday being his deception and lies and other women. I held it in and tried to cope by praying and focusing on the prize of becoming a RN in a few months. The only thing that brightened my days, were my kids and my belief that *"and this, too, shall pass."*

The Poorest of Timing

I was pregnant. Second year of Nursing School, among all the drama and unhappiness at home, it happened. I was due in May of 1998. Was it a mistake or was it intentional? I was so confused and stuck on stupid when it came to Kenny, I really couldn't tell you. Kenny seemed happy. Probably because it gave him security in knowing that I wasn't leaving him, and that we could have a new baby to start over new. I continued to go to school and work at the Insurance Agency. Managing to keep my head up even with everyone knowing my family woes and problems. One day I made an appointment with the Dean of my Nursing School, and while waiting in the hall I just broke down. I cried so hard, I was glad the building was practically empty. I cried and I cried. By the time the Dean saw me, I blurted out "I'm pregnant." She comforted me and gave me my options. I could try and finish the next Semester due to end Mid-May and graduate with my Class early June. Or I could take a semester leave and return in September and Graduate in January. I wouldn't be able to participate in the actual Candle lighting and Graduation until the entire class graduated late May. I opted to take a leave. I was mentally and physically exhausted. My man was expecting two babies six months apart, and the financial burden of the court cases was still very evident in my home finances.

I was able to put in more hours at the Insurance Agency. And I tried to think positive, but I was disgusted with myself. Kenny and I decided to finally get married. I had mixed emotions. On one hand, I felt that I had fought the good fight and kept my family from falling apart and getting married was the final step in sealing our commitment. And on the other hand, I wondered if it was all worth it. *"Will Kenny finally recognize that his family is the most important priority in his life? And finally, be the man that I saw he was capable of being?"*

Here I was, pregnant, tired, taking time off of school, he had no income the months he was off of work, we couldn't pay our bills, and I was driving a raggedy mini truck with no back seats to keep my children safe. *"What more could I take? What more could I do to prove that I was down for my family?"*

A few weeks later, I found a favor from S's Baby Shower. Here Kenny was telling me he wanted a blood test, but going to the baby shower? It made no sense. He said Kenny's sister went and brought it back to him. Oh, so, she can go to S's Baby Shower, but didn't go to mines for Shayna? I had a friend visiting from out of town. Shara was staying with me a few days and she had to witness all this mess. I cussed Kenny's sister out as she sat in her car in my driveway. I told her she was a miserable bitch, a liar, two-faced, and jealous of me being in the family. She had me thinking that she was finally being a friend to me when she was deceitful. I had no idea that she and S were friends. I was hurt that she didn't show me any type of love when I was pregnant with Shayna, but she was going out of her way for the side chick. I was so tired of being lied to. I didn't care if they were friends, but I cared that I wasn't made aware of it so that I would know not to trust her.

Kenny got cussed out, too. Shara and I went out that weekend to Puff Daddy's party in New York City. I was not showing yet, and I had a good time. Shara always had my back, and although she had no idea of what I had been through in the past few months, I didn't share that another female was pregnant. I just wanted to enjoy my friend without Kenny's wrongs being the main subject for once. I was mad at myself for letting Shara see me cussing folks out. She just knew that if I was cussing people out, I had a good reason

Love & Happiness

I wanted to be married on Christmas Eve. I had always wanted to get married on Christmas Eve, it was one of those fantasies I had when I was younger. As we began to plan and prepare, I was working with a very tight budget. Cynthia, A and

Lisa were right there with me. I wanted to get married in the same church where Kenny's big Brother's Funeral was held. It is a beautiful church, with wooden pews and Cathedral ceilings. Kenny called to book the wedding, and was told "No" at first because of the Holiday. Several hours later, the Pastor called back and agreed, saying that his wife thought it was a beautiful idea.

As I made plans, I missed my family even more. The wedding would only be two months away, and I knew that it would be difficult for anyone to make it. It would be a small, intimate wedding with only people who love us present. I expected less than 100 people.

I found a dress that I liked and thought could be altered to accommodate my growing belly. And I put the deposit down so that it could be ordered. Angie and Lisa were with me when I picked I out at a Bridal Store in New Jersey. As the wedding grew nearer I was busy making favors, flower arrangements, and planning the menu for the very small reception, which would be at our home. Angie and Lisa began to share with me all of the things that Kenny's sister had been saying and doing to me over the past years. They were upset that she was not helping me at all, when they saw how I had helped her for her wedding and birth of her second child.

Kenny's sister had told anyone and everyone she could that I was lazy, didn't clean my house, was insanely jealous of her "poor, innocent brother", and an all-around "Bitch." But, she slipped up, and when these people and her in-laws, who would later also confirm all of the things Kenny's sister had been saying falsely about me, saw me in action and spent time with me, they learned otherwise. And EVERYTHING Kenny's sister said about me, was now being said about her! And these were people who knew her for years. Kenny's sister was the one that did not clean her house, Kenny's sister was the user, Kenny's sister was the "Bitch", and Kenny's sister was doing her best to sabotage anything good that was happening in my life. And with the accusations of Rape and the other child on the way, everyone now knew that Kenny was not the honest, respectable brother Kenny's sister made him out to be.

When I asked Cynthia to be my Maid of Honor, she was concerned about backlash from the family because of all that was going on with Kenny's sister. Kenny's Mom thought Kenny's sister should have been included in our wedding! And when I told her parents all of the things Kenny's sister had been saying and doing, their response was, "That's just Kenny's sister." Kenny's sister's response was, "I'm sorry that I had friends who would betray me."

Reasons to Smile, and Reasons to Cry

Angie and Lisa convinced me and the kids to spend the weekend out in New Jersey in Early November. It was Veteran's Day weekend, so there was no school on Monday. I told them I did not want a Bridal Shower or Party because the wedding was such short notice, and I didn't want to put any one in a financial strain. I was overwhelmed with planning and making everything for the wedding. So, they told me they just wanted to have dinner and they would keep it very small and inexpensive. We would be spending the night and having a small slumber party. I drove out to Jersey early Friday evening. And was supposed to go and do the last sizing and pick my wedding dress up the next day.

Angie and Lisa had a big box waiting for me. I cried when I opened the box. It was my Wedding Dress! They had put their money together and paid the remainder on the dress. Somehow, they convinced the Saleslady to let them do that! I was so touched. I couldn't believe they would do such a nice thing for me. Later, they would tell me they felt so bad for allowing Kenny's sister to influence their opinions of me in the beginning that they wanted to do something nice for me.

When the weekend was over I drove back to Staten Island. Kennith looked worried. He sat me down on the couch in the living room and told me that S, pregnant with K's baby had the baby. I didn't ask any questions. I just listened. There weren't any details. It was a boy. I felt numb.

I cried in my room, alone. So many things went through my head. I wondered if the weekend away had been planned to get me out of town. I wondered if Kenny was there holding her the way he held me when Shayna was born. It hurt, and I felt guilt for being hurt. I prayed and I asked God to help me to love this baby the way God loves him. I did not want to feel animosity for a baby. Yes, it hurt. Yes, I wished it didn't happen. But, it did happen. And it was not the baby's fault. I promised God I would treat him the way I would want my son treated.

It took a lot of prayer and asking God to help me to be forgiving and to do what was right, even when it didn't feel good. I encouraged Kennith to be a Father. I had no idea how he was going to do it. But, I needed to know that he was a man who would take care of all of his kids, not just the ones by me. I had went shopping for my kids, I learned to shop on a budget and knew how to make the most out of sales so I picked up some things for a little boy. Kennith would not give them to the baby. He had me under the impression that he was not in contact with S, or the baby. That was not for my benefit, it was never what I wanted.

And so, at home, Kennith acted like his son didn't exist. That thought troubled me. I was never with a man ignoring his children. I did not think that our family would be blessed if he didn't take care of his children, all of his children.

For Better, What Could Be Worse?

Our wedding day approached. Cynthia and I were busy cooking and preparing the food for the small reception. Kennith's parents had come to town for the wedding. I was trying to keep the house clean and tidy, and prepare for the guests. It was very difficult with a house full of people. Kenny's Mother had asked me why I chose to have the wedding on Christmas Eve, "People want to be with their family on Christmas Eve." Was how she put it. "And weddings are for family and loved ones to be together, also." Was my response.

I had asked Kenny if I could have the house to myself the night before the wedding. I wanted him and Marcel to go and spend the night somewhere and Shayna, Cynthia and I to be at my house so I could unwind and finish the preparations. His Mother was angry that I wanted to be by myself; I guess they felt put out. I never intended that, I just wanted to be in a calm atmosphere as I prepared. His parents went to Kenny's sister's house, and Kenny, Marcel and V, the Best Man spent the night at Cynthia's house.

The next day was full of preparations. The cake had gotten smashed on the way home. I was able to save it, and it was a beautiful small cake decorated with gold and white flowers. The food all looked good, and was plentiful. I had decorated the Christmas tree with hand-decorated ornaments in Gold, Red, and Ivory, which would be given away as the keepsake favors for the guests.

was supposed to sing, but had Bronchitis and couldn't. The Keyboardist's wife filled in and sang. Kenny surprised me with a Limousine, his friend at work drove them part-time and he got a discount because God knows we could barely afford any extras.

Cynthia and I still laugh because as soon as the limo pulled off, she popped a piece of gum into her mouth. I asked for a piece, and she stopped chewing and just looked at me. We stared at each other for a moment and then she took the gum out of her mouth and we both laughed. "If you really need it!" she laughed, and I really needed it. So, I put the gum in my mouth, "Now, this is love!" We laughed all the way to the church.

It was a small group of those we loved, and as the songstress sung Babyface's "Every time I close my Eyes." Shayna and Marcel began to walk out of the foyer. Shayna looked at all the people, cried and turned around and ran right back to my arms. Everyone laughed. Her Uncle Anthony got her to try again, and this time she walked a few steps holding her big brother's hand, and then she saw her Daddy and ran down the aisle crying to him. He picked her up and Marcel continued his Mh down the aisle to where his Dad stood.

I walked in alone. And made my way to where my family stood. The church had Red Poinsettia's decorating the pulpit and the aisles. It was beautiful. Snow lightly fell outside, and Kenny and I became husband and wife. We jumped the broom and made our way back down the aisle and out to the Limo for the trip back to our home.

Christmas Eve 1997 at St Phillips Church, Staten Island.

We laughed, and we talked, and everyone ate and drank. Of course, Kenny smashed me with cake, and we had our customary cake fight. His aunt had sent a red velvet cake all the way from down south with his parents, and we would not dare waste that one on a cake fight. Kenny's sister, came about three hours late. No matter what she and I had been through, she could have shown more respect for her brother.

I took my vows seriously. We were in it forever, and I had hopes of us living happily after ever. I loved him. And I loved my family. And we had a chance to make it. I believed in us. After all we had been through; I felt that we had an opportunity to rise above and make our family stronger.

Baby Love

Kennith Michael Moorer, Jr. was born May 2nd, 1998. I had stopped working Friday, May 1st. And was having what I thought were Braxton Hicks Contractions all day. Kenny came in from work, and I told him that I felt strange. After a couple of hours, I called him in from outside where he was working on a car. I thought I was in labor, even though the baby wasn't due for another three weeks. A few hours passed, and the pains were stronger and more consistent. I realized I really was in labor and realized that we had nobody to watch the kids. Cynthia and Anthony were out of town. And even though I didn't like her, so was Kenny's sister. A lived over an hour away. Kim had moved back to Pennsylvania, and Ronique was not available. Kenny called V and had him on his way to Staten Island from Red Hook. My pains were intense and I was scared. As we waited for V, the pains increased in strength and intensity. When V reached the Staten Island Terminal and was walking to get in a Taxi, we sat Marcel who was 8 and Shayna who was 4 on the couch. We gave Marcel the phone and told him to talk to his Dad, and to open the door only for V. As we drove to the hospital we were about fifteen minutes from the hospital when Kenny heard the knock on the door through the phone. He told Marcel to open the door and once he confirmed V was there he hung up.

My nurse Mid-wife was supposed to deliver my son. I had wanted to try the natural route, but God had other plans. The baby was not in the proper position; there was no way I could deliver vaginally. I was so upset that I had waited so long to go in, I could have avoided all that pain if I had gone in earlier in the day. The Doctor was called in, and I was given an epidural and prepared for a C-Section delivery. Kenny stood next to me over my left shoulder. I began to feel the incision and told Kenny, "I can feel that." Then I yelled, "It hurts." I started to vomit, and

Kenny held up a canister for me. The anesthesiologist heard me, and put a mask over my face. I was sedated, and I couldn't move or talk. But, I heard every word that was said, and I felt the Doctor and the Resident pulling and tugging. I heard when the baby came out, and I felt them when they were sewing me back up.

It would be hours before I was able to hold and feed my son. Kennith Jr., looked just like his father. We boned with our baby that night, and when the Doctor came in the next day to tell me that I would have to have a Cesarean if I ever had another baby because of the extent of the incision, I told him that I felt and heard everything.

Healing from the Cesarean was no joke. Kenny brought us home and then went to pick up the kids. Kenny would always clean he house from top to bottom and cook a good dinner whenever we brought a baby home. KJ and I were upstairs when Shayna and Marcel ran in and saw KJ in his bassinette. They were very excited to have a little brother.

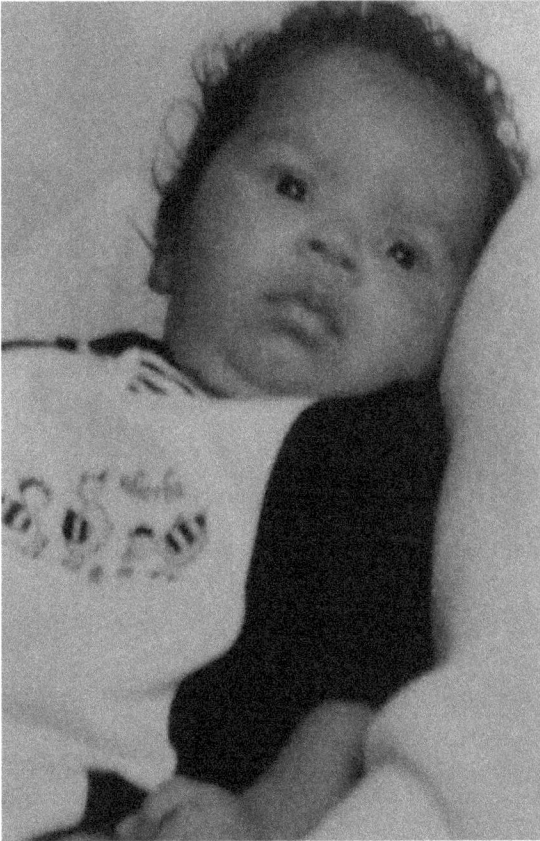

Kennith Michael Moorer, Jr. was born May 2nd, 1998.

Back at It

Kenny and S, had been in child support court for months, and Kennith had to pay over $700.00 a month. With back child support increasing that to over $1500 a month being deducted from his checks. But, I had married him knowing full well of what was ahead, so I tried to ride with him. He complained that he wasn't able to see him or be a father, so he decided to file for visitation. He would have to spend several hours with S and the baby boy at a mutual location. What bothered me was, Kenny worked five days a week including Saturday, and now his Sundays would be spent away from our kids so that he could bond with the baby. It would have benefited all of the kids much more if the baby could have come to our house and be with the entire family, but his Mother refused.

Our household suffered, bills were not getting paid, and we were barely making ends meet. I tried to have Kenny's back, but, it was very difficult.

In July, Kenny's sister was planning her son's 1st birthday party. We received our invitation, and then Kenny gave me some news. Kenny's sister had invited S, and the baby. And Kenny had found out from S, or so he the child. This created an uncomfortable situation. And I was angry because Kenny's sister should have told me. Instead I felt like my children and I were being set up. Everyone else knew what to expect, but us. She knew it would be a very awkward and possibly ugly situation I was blindly walking into.

I decided to meet with S. Without Kennith knowing it, I called her and asked if we could meet. We met at the park. We were polite. I explained to her why I wanted her to meet me. Our kids are siblings, and I wanted her to be comfortable that someday her son would be around us. She asked me if I wanted to know details about her and Kenny. And I told her that my knowing they had a son together was details enough, my imagination could fill in the blanks. She said that she didn't know that I was in the dark about the birthday party. I told her that I truly did not care if she and Kenny's sister were friends. Kenny's sister's true colors would shine through soon enough, and as long as she was not in my business I was glad that she was in someone else's. I told her that I hoped she knew I would only want what was best for her son, and that I would treat him the way I would want her to treat my kids.

The meeting didn't help with Kenny's visitation rights, and eventually Kenny would stop attempting all together. I never wanted that. But, I was powerless in the situation. Kenny's sister continued to try and interfere, but I cared less and less. I had enough on my plate, and no matter how hard I wanted to try and do what was right by all of the kids, I couldn't do it alone.

When God Sends Help

It was time for me to return and complete my last semester of Nursing School. KJ was only 4 months old, Shayna was almost 5, and Marcel was almost 9. We continued to struggle financially.   After all of the ups and downs, K seemed more in tune with his family. I hoped that he had enough of running around and saw that he was given another chance to be the husband and father I believed he could be. I had stuck with him, continued to love him and carried on. I was hurt, never really healing from the previous year's events. But, I was committed to my family.

In order to return to school, I had to have no debts to the school, and I was unable to pay a bill of $1800 from St Johns. I was in a hole, and could not see a way out. I went to my Dean and told her my circumstances. I cried. She must have thought I was really having problems, this was the second time I had bawled my eyes out in her office. She gave me hope. She told me that if I could pay the $1800 to St. Johns, then they would release my credits and that she would give me a Scholarship to complete my last semester! God always came through and gave me just enough. I called my Mom and my sisters, they contributed a couple hundred, we scraped and I pawned some jewelry and I started my last semester.

Cynthia would watch KJ in the Insurance office while I was at school. I would go in after school and on weekends and work. KJ became a part of the atmosphere, with the clients asking for him, bringing him things and helping to take care of him. It was like God always made a way out of no way. I had found another sitter for Marcel and Shayna, and continued to receive the babysitting grant from the city so I could finish school. Looking back, I could say I don't know how I did it, "But God!"

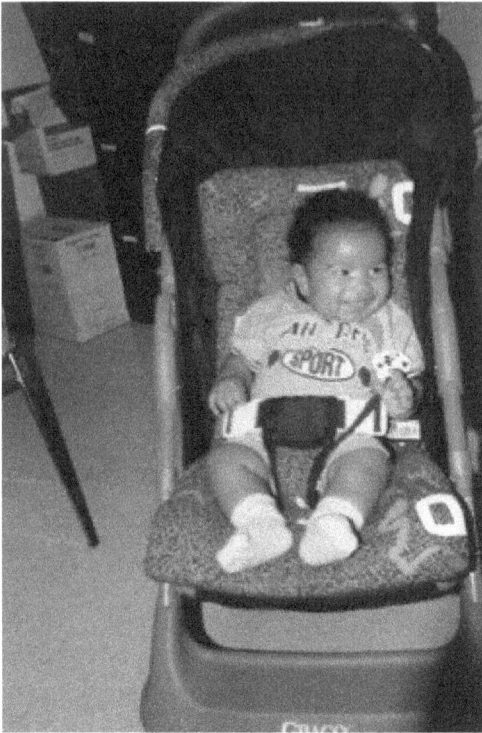

KJ being taken care of by Cynthia at Bryson Insurance while I was in Nursing School.

I finished in January of 1999. Graduation would not be for another six months, and it would be with another class, but I did it. I passed my NCLEX on the first try. I was a Registered Nurse. I loved having those initials behind my name. It gave me such a confidence. I was so proud of myself. K and the kids looked proud during my Candle-lighting Ceremony and Graduation a few months later. My first job was a Private Duty job providing care to a young man with a debilitating disease. I took it because K and I had started plans to move down south. I was so ready for a new atmosphere, and I believe K was trying to run from some things. Either way, all I could think about was that I would be closer to California. I knew I needed hospital experience, but if we had an opportunity to move I would leave and I didn't want to commit to a hospital at that time.

My Graduation Day from St. Vincent's School of Nursing.

K's parents were glad that we planned to move down south; of course, they wanted family near them. They were also relieved because with all of K's legal problems they had to loan him a lot of money and help us out a lot. I appreciated it. I really did, I just hoped that they knew it was his problems and I supported him through it. It had been a long hard road, but I was no longer allowing Kenny's sister to dictate how we all got along. I just ignored her, and Kenny's parents and I were getting along fine. The loved us, and they were always willing to help the kids and would spoil them when they could.

We had bought a used Bronco, and I was comfortable with it. I didn't have a car payment, and the kids fit comfortably in it. After having to drive around unsafely in the Nissan Truck, I was relieved to have a reliable car. Kenny made the sudden decision to drive the Bronco down South to get his Mother so that she could see a Doctor in New York. I did not have a say, and although I understood that he wanted to help his Mother, I didn't understand how it was necessary. His parents spent plenty of time in New York, and it made more sense for her to fly to New York if she were not feeling well. Either way, Kenny left with a day's notice and drove to Florida. Kenny returned with his Mother several days later. I was informed that the engine blew on my Bronco and that I would be paying his parents $300 a month for their used Ford Explorer. I had no choice. I was upset, but it was just one more of Kenny's decisions that I had to live with.

They put the house on Vanderbilt up for sale and we planned to move. Kenny applied for a transfer, and those are hard to get in the Post office without losing seniority. The Postmaster in Alabama helped after we went down and met with him. The house sold before we could make the move down south, so we moved into a small apartment in a two-family home under Shawn and Dorilys. They were family, and they had a house full of kids. Living underneath them was a very loud and activity filled time, but it was filled with fun.

Kenny and the kids in the small apartment we rented on the first floor of a two-story home in Staten Island.

By Mh of 2000, we had moved in with his parents in Pensacola, Florida. I found a job in Mobile, Alabama at USA Hospital. We stayed with his parents a few months and then moved into a house in the Forest Hills section of Mobile, Alabama. I worked nights 7p to 7a, and K worked days 8 to 5 with a lot of overtime. He would be with the kids at night, and I would take care of KJ during the day, and get the kids to and from school. Sometimes, one of Kenny's little cousins, Kim, would come and babysit the kids for us. The house had a huge backyard, and was tri-level. We had a nice sized den downstairs.

The Living room, kitchen and dining area were on the first floor. K turned the Living room into a studio. I thought we were finally going to be happy. The kids were in good schools. We had a chance for a fresh new start. It would be awhile before I realized that bitterness was building. I wanted to see remorse from K. I wanted to have him look at me the way he had so many years ago in my Mother's Living Room. I wanted him to fight to keep his beautiful family. I wanted him to appreciate that I was riding with him. I wanted to really believe that he would rebuild all the trust that was lost in New York. And I continued to believe that once we had survived enough negative, once I had jumped enough hurdles, and once we overcame one more barrier that we would be healthy and happy and un-breakable. I believed that the hard times were making us stronger.

Same Old Shit

I had a good job, it taught me a lot. The nurses I worked with were some of the best. They trained me well. I was exhausted most of the time from caring for KJ during the day and working at night. I would sleep trying to get my body enough rest to carry on. Kenny continued to DJ. He was in his studio a lot. Eventually, I enrolled KJ in a daycare next to the kid's elementary school. This helped some, but working night shift ain't no joke.

The kids posing for our yearly Christmas photo on the porch of the house in the Forest Hill Section of Mobile, Alabama.

Shayna met a little friend in Kindergarten named Christie. She lived right up the street, and I met her mother. Valeria ended up being one of my best friends. She has such a warm and caring attitude; she is very giving and fun. This helped me to cope. I found a good church and me and the kids would attend when I wasn't working.

Months passed, and by this time, I was so eager to begin a new life I wasn't watching K. I wasn't checking his phone, or looking for anything. But, it found its way to me; some random broad, again and again and again. I even found text messages between Kennith and his best friend's wife (and I was not looking for them). They lived in California, and Kenny had stayed in their home during one of his visits there. The messages were explicit and included facts that couldn't be denied. In one text he was telling her how he liked fucking her in her husband's bed!. This was the last straw. I was done. I think he saw a difference in me. He cried, he even dedicated the song *"Love"* by Musiq Soulchild to me over the radio one morning.

Too late, I was already done. I had been riding for him thru good and bad, and I finally realized I was not willing to die for him.

As things between Kenny and I deteriorated, I began to work on building myself back up. I hated paying for and driving that Explorer I had been forced to purchase. I stopped paying for it. I told Kenny that he made the decision to buy it, and he needed to be the one to pay for it. One day, Val and I drove to the Ford Dealership and I bought a Brand-New Ford Explorer. I traded the old Explorer in, I never wanted it and I resented having to pay for it for over a year. Just one more situation where we would all disagree on what went down, who was right, and who was wrong.

We sought counseling. It was useless. You can't counsel a liar. I was tired of being ignored, and I was tired of my kids being ignored. He should have been spending his time rebuilding his family, not chasing bitches. I told him I wanted a divorce. I wanted to move back to California, and he agreed. Of course, he only agreed when I succumbed to only $200 every pay period in child support. For 3 kids, or for 2, since technically he had no legal obligation to Marcel. I did resent the fact that his having to pay child support to S, pregnant with K's baby reduced any amount my kids would ever receive. So, here I would be getting $400 a month for 2 kids! It just didn't seem fair. It seemed like I was being punished for staying and trying to work things out. Like, oh well, she filed first so you and your kids gotta make it the best you can.

Around this time, a cute resident showed up at USA. All the nurses flirted with him. I didn't. I was not interested in anything but getting out of Alabama.

He began to flirt with me, though and it peaked my interest. I tried ignoring him. Then one day he caught me at the end of the hall, and asked if I would hang out with him. He said he wanted to play pool or have drinks. "I would have called you last night if I had your number." My response was, "You know my name. I'm sure you can figure out how to get my number." The next day was Friday, and he called my home phone. He must have got my number from the hospital staff directory, I never asked. I gave him my cell number, and we planned a date. I had Val get my kids and we met up at a Movie Theatre way in West Mobile.

Then we had drinks and appetizers at Applebee's. It felt good

not to have to beg for attention. ` Plus, he was FINE and SMART.

I needed somebody to uplift my spirits and remind me that I was

still valuable to a man.

We talked and spent another day or two together over the

next few weeks. It was wearing on me, because I already had a

busy schedule and I was also preparing a divorce and relocation.

I was so hurt and angry with K. He had moved us way out to

Alabama for a fresh start, and ends up putting women before his

family, again. I was fed up. I ended up having an affair with that

young resident that lasted until I left for California. It was a

sweet release, although wrong.

K found out about my affair. He went through my phone,

I thought I was slick and had him listed under "USA Resident"

but apparently, I wasn't slick enough. He called the Doctor's

phone one day and because he was in surgery, a nurse answered

and took a message. K left the message, "Call Rayna Moorer." I

had no idea Kenny had called him until the Doctor called me and asked me what I needed thinking it was some kind of emergency. Kenny had the nerve to be mad. He was running around Mobile with random chicken-heads and he was mad at me! But this time, I didn't give a damn.

Home, Sweet Home?

K helped us pack for California; we rented a U-Haul and drove my Ford Explorer back to Cali. We got along enough to avoid arguing on the trip, until I heard him making plans for a different trip. I was mad. He always found money to do what he wanted, but the kids and I were always sacrificing.

The kids and I were going to stay with my sister, Karla, for a few months until I got my own place. I had a travel nurse assignment at Kaiser arranged and I was starting a brand-new life. Before Kenny left, I gave in and we had sex one last time on the floor when no one was home.

I planned my new life as a single Mother. Kaiser was the most miserable place I ever worked for. The nurses were mean, and they were extra mean to travel nurses. Home was stressful, also. My sister was a clean freak, and a control freak, so I was miserable at her house. I cried every day because my marriage was over. I was so angry with myself for still loving him. I was angry with him for continuing to be an asshole. And I was angry with God because no matter how hard I prayed, my family had fallen apart. There were days when I was so depressed I would pull over and cry on the way to work, and then again on the way home. I was working as a Travel-Nurse for Kaiser in Fontana, and that was a horrible experience. The other nurses were not nice. I was often left to fend for myself in unknown territory. No matter what Nursing skills you have, if you do not know where to find this or that, or if there is no one available to help you turn a patient, if no one offers to assist you, it is impossible to work. If I hadn't had the skills and the personality I have, I would have quit working there the first week.

I thought I was going to have a breakdown. One morning I drove to the drug store and waited until they opened. I bought a pregnancy test and found out I was pregnant. My depression deepened. I missed work. I was vomiting all over the place. I was miserable. I did not want a baby. When I told Kenny, he said he wanted me to have an abortion. I refused. I never believed abortion would ever be right for me. I didn't believe he wanted me to really have an abortion at the time. But, thinking about it now, he might have really wanted me to have one. Either way, I would never abort a child.

I felt so sick, nauseated, tired, and depressed all of the time. I focused on rebuilding my life and being a Single-Mom. Shayna's Birthday was approaching, and I asked her what she wanted. During those first few weeks in Cali I tried to teach the kids to call their Dad just to say "Hi." And to see how he was doing. I did not want them in the habit of only calling him when they wanted something. So, when Shayna said she wanted to tell her Dad what she wanted for her Birthday as I was rushing out the door for work, I rehearsed having the same speech with her again to enforce that she has to call him all the time, not just to ask for things.

The next day I sat down with Shayna to help her to call her Daddy. I asked her what she wanted to ask him for, and she said, "All I want is for my Daddy to come and see me for my Birthday." It brought tears to my eyes. Shayna had always been a Daddy's girl and I knew she missed him, probably more than I missed him. Shayna called her Daddy and asked him to come visit. Kenny and I talked afterwards and made plans for him to fly in for the weekend. I arranged a weekend at Disneyland, and we celebrated Shayna's Birthday as a family.

We discussed getting back together, but didn't have any concrete plans. My Mother wanted me to move into her small Condo and stay in California. I wanted to go back to Kenny. Of course, I was afraid. But, I just wanted my husband. I didn't know what to do.

I began bleeding profusely, and I thought I was going to lose the baby that I didn't want in the first place. When it really looked like I really would lose the baby, I realized that I wanted it. K and I talked often and he asked me what I needed. I told him I needed rest. I was overwhelmed, I was breaking down and I didn't know if I could get it together. I was afraid. The last few years had taken its toll. I just wanted to feel safe, and I wanted to rest.

K flew out to Cali in February and brought us and our things back home. Once again, we were staying with his parents. He let me rest. I saw love in his eyes again, and I thought it was going to get better. Being away from Kenny was hard, I could not get over wanting my husband, wanting my marriage to work, and wanting my kids to be in a two-parent home. Again, I was convinced that Kenny had learned his lesson and that he had realized that he wanted all of the same things.

Once in Alabama, I saw a Doctor that was recommended and he performed a pelvic exam and began to take care of my pregnancy. We discovered that the bleeding had been due to the miscarriage of a twin. Once the fetus was removed the bleeding stopped and the high-risk pregnancy continued. I couldn't work, I couldn't pay any of my bills, and my disability barely covered my car note. My bills went unpaid and my credit suffered, badly. K had filed bankruptcy during our divorce, so his credit was on the upswing. I figured I would focus on his so we could buy a home, at least one of us would have good credit and my credit would suffer. And it did.

We bought a cute little house in the Lake Forest Subdivision in Daphne. We moved in when I was five months pregnant. It didn't need much work, and it had a small office in the middle of the backyard K would use for a studio. The kids had good schools to attend, and we all waited for our last baby to be born.

Myles Gerald Moorer

Myles Gerald Moorer was born by Cesarean Section on August 12th, 2002. And my tubes were tied so I couldn't have any more children. Myles was adorable. The kids were just in awe with him, Shayna especially. She was like a little Mother to him. She would bathe him, change him, and feed him. When I eventually returned to Nursing, she would take care of him and allow me to sleep. I found a Nursing Position at Mobile Infirmary. Working night shift again. We needed money, and the night shift meant I didn't have to pay childcare.

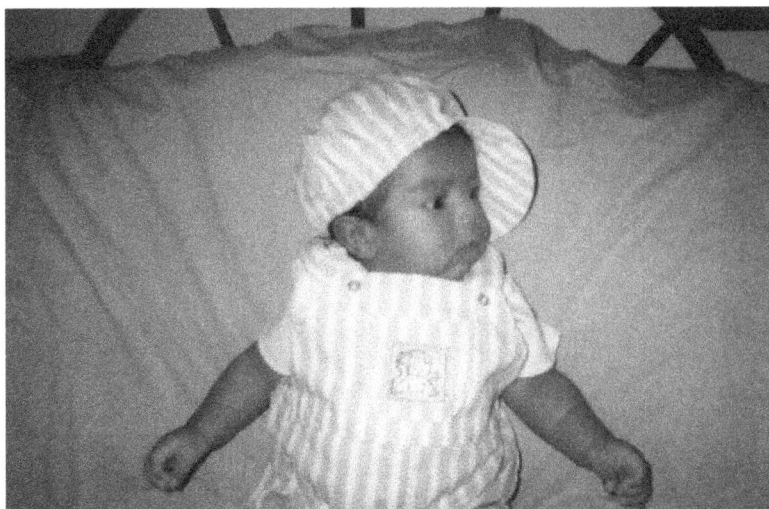

Myles Gerald Moorer, born August 12, 2002.

Shortly after Myles' birth, my sister, Trish, and her kids were living in Michigan with her youngest daughter's father. We were in communication, and she was unhappy. She asked if they could come live with us. I missed my family terribly, and wanted to help so K drove to Saginaw, Michigan to get them. They moved in, and though I appreciated the help with Myles and the kids. It tuned bad quickly. I was very aggravated with hearing about all the things her man had done for her, how good he was to her, how she missed him. But, yet I was feeding her whole family and buying her baby diapers. I bought them train tickets and sent them back to California.

Myles was quiet and calm most of the time. But, he had the worse colic of all my babies. I would pace the floor with him many nights, trying to quiet him. Shortly after Myles' birth Kenny returned to DJ'ing for Lyte. I was glad that he returned to something that I knew he had missed for so long. I felt he was very worthy of finally getting what he deserved from Lyte. I hoped that he would focus more on the family once he was given the opportunity to do what he loved again.

Kennith, Myles and I in our home in Daphne, Alabama. Kenny was leaving for an out of town gig.

Finding My Calling

While working at the Infirmary my Supervisor asked me to become a member of the Palliative Care Team. As member of the team we were educated and received extra training regarding proving care of terminally ill patients. I fit in well, and excelled as a Palliative Care Nurse. I resigned after working there for two years to seek a daytime position with a Hospice Agency that was closer to my home. I was hired as a RN Case Manager with Covenant Hospice in Daphne, Alabama. I loved it. The company was dedicated to providing the best Hospice Care, they valued their staff and our office was intimate and close-knit. My Branch Manager and Nursing Supervisor were appreciative and understanding of a Mother's and family needs. I received excellent training, and the Medical Director was down to earth, professional and supportive. I was very happy with that job. I took about a $5 an hour pay cut, but with overtime and after-hours call pay I was able to make it. The kids were growing and participating in school. KJ played football, Marcel got a job, and Shayna became a Cheerleader. We were a busy family.

My Sisters in California and I would experience division at its worst during this time. My oldest sister confided something in me that would affect the entire family. I felt that keeping it in confidence would be more harmful and I shared it with my other sister. This caused everything to fall apart. We all argued and my oldest sister stopped speaking to me. There had always been some level of division between us in various forms. But, this was the first time it was aimed at me. I had always managed to maintain relationships with each of them, even if they were not getting along with each other. It had always seemed I was exempt. I didn't know how to take it. I felt that I had done the right thing, and I was so mad. I had come to realize a lot about my sisters over the years. Much of it left me disappointed. I had put them on pedestals. I always felt that they would protect me, and the situation showed me that I was not going to always be treated like the "Little Sister." Our roles had changed, and I was not happy with it. I thought that we had all survived the dysfunction of our childhood, and the older I became the more dysfunction I saw. I never wanted to see any of it. I wanted to stay the hopeful little sister. I was angry that they took away my imaginary family and replaced it with the real one that I could no longer pretend was not there.

Depression would peak it's head out at me at intervals. I tried to fight it. Our marriage was still failing. I craved his attention, and did not get it. Insecurities crept in, and my weight crept up and up after the birth of Myles. There were so many signs that K was still womanizing. Yet, if I questioned him, I was nagging him. And if I withdrew, then he used that as an excuse for not being at home. The kids were growing up, and as Shayna reached the age of eleven she withdrew from her Dad. I saw it happening, and I tried to reinforce that she needed her Dad's attention. Everything I said was taken negatively. We didn't talk; we fought. I felt like I was fighting for my life. Depression took over and I was not only fighting Depression, but had been diagnosed with Diabetes for several years. Lack of proper care, emotional strain, and depression took a hold of my life. I was tearful a lot and sadness overtook me.

Disneyland, California on a
family vacation in 2004.

I constantly felt bad that Kenny did not have a
relationship with Kenny's other son.. I felt guilty, and it scared
me to think that if he could do that to her child, he could to it to
mine. We would argue on and off about Kenny's other son.. I
would buy him gifts, and K would refuse to send them. Then one
day I go the news that Kenny's other son. had been sick. He had
a life-threatening illness and I approached K. I asked him about
it, and he told me what was going on, well what little he knew
about it. We argued and I insisted that he tell our kids about
Kenny's other son.. One day he sat the kids down and told them

they had a brother. I knew that I had to be strong, because if they saw me upset about it they would be upset about it. I stood strong and made sure the kids knew that I was caring and loving of their brother. The kids began to contact each other once we cleared it with the child's Mohter. I was so relieved. I hated family secrets; they lead to nothing but more heartache and confusion.

We would drive to New York a few months later and the kids would meet one another. The child's Mother. was polite, invited us all into her home and allowed us to spend time with Kenny's other son. who was about six by then. She let us take him to Six Flags, and we all had a good time. I hoped that Kenny's other son. would never feel like he wasn't wanted. From then on, I would buy him clothes, birthday presents, and cards and send them to him from Kenny and the kids.

Kennith and I grew further apart. We would fight often. He had a friend, some female who came up out of nowhere. He claimed they were "Best Friends." Yes, I was jealous. Here I was craving the attention of a very busy man, the last thing he needed was a female, "Best Friend." Eventually we met, and I just did not click with her. I tried, but I did not like it. I found out that she had a baby, and I once teased K saying that the child was very light, and both she and her husband were dark skinned. My husband told her what I said. And the fact that he was quick to betray me to others told me plenty about what he thought of me.

Once, we had to go down to the courthouse to file charges against a man who tried to intrude in our house. We had to sit and complete our complaint with the Magistrate. A few days later, K lay across my bed on the phone with his cousin telling him how he used to have sex with the woman. *"Here we go again. Geez, is there any female you haven't had sex with? Anyone who doesn't know somebody you been having sex with?"* I became paranoid. Thinking that every woman I met knew some secret about me, or had been sleeping with my husband.

I began to tune out the signs of adultery. I tried to focus on praying and being more positive. I began seeing a counselor again, when Marcel was having difficulty in school. Marcel longed to be in California, he would cry himself to sleep repeating, *"I want to be in Cal...i...forn...ia."* It would just break my heart. The counseling helped Marcel, and me and I looked for a counselor for myself. It helped. I began to see how I was allowing myself to be miserable. I couldn't blame Kenny for everything. I played a huge part in my circumstance. I would have to focus on myself and my children and let God deal with Kenny. I didn't know how, but at least I received the revelation that put me in search of the right answers.

My niece came to spend the summer with us when Shayna was about eleven. I was glad to have her visiting. But, with the strain between Kenny and I it made me feel even worse that we weren't getting along. Shayna just reminded me recently that her Dad and I were arguing, and he put me in the closet and held the door closed for a long time. She told me how this scared her and my niece, and how we fought a lot when we lived in the house in Daphne. It's strange how most of those years have become a blur. I can recall dates and situations that happened in New York, but much of the bad stuff that happened in Daphne escapes me. I do know I was very unhappy, and I do know I was searching for God.

My goals seemed to shift from trying to make my marriage work, to trying to figure out why I was so unhappy. I began to realize that K was not completely to blame for my unhappiness. He had his issues, I had my issues and together we had compounded issues.

Seek & You Shall Find

The loneliness in that house was unbearable. I was lonely in a room full of people. My heart ached. The love of my kids was the only bright spots for the three years we lived in that house. The kids and I spent a lot of time at church. I began to feel God working in my life. It was a process and I could barely feel it, but I felt it. And it gave me a glimmer of hope.

I had been noticing that Myles was not like my other kids. He was not meeting the landmarks in development as my other three had. He did not speak, ever. He would point, and he would find a way to tell me what he wanted sometimes. But, his communication was poor. He understood some things. He was behind about three months with sitting up, crawling, and walking.

I was afraid to send him to Daycare, so Val's mother took care of him during the day. He didn't walk until he was 16 months, when all my other kids were walking before the age of one. I would ask his Pediatrician, and I would be told, "He's a boy," or "He will be fine" or "He's the Baby of the Family. He will talk eventually." I watched him closely. I researched Autism, asking myself if I those were the signs I was seeing. He fit some, but not the determinant signs of Autism.

When he turned three years old, I made an appointment with his Pediatrician. It just so happened, that his Pediatrician was not in and Myles was seen by his wife. She agreed with my concerns and got the ball rolling to have him referred for further examinations. He had extensive hearing tests, was referred to a Neurologist, had MRI's, saw Speech Therapists, and had some Genetics Testing performed. They found nothing. He obviously had Speech and Developmental Delays. But, it was not Autism. I called a number I saw at my children's school that asked if your child had signs of delay to call, and I did. That got the ball rolling for the school district to begin testing and placement. Myles was able to attend Special Education Preschool. No one could ever give us a diagnosis, or tell us why he was not developing as he should.

There were times I wished it was Autism. At least then we could get more help. I took him to three different Neurologist and Developmental Specialists. They could only tell me something was wrong with his Brain, but they didn't know what. That was a fight with the Insurance Company; if there is no diagnosis there are no codes to dictate what your child is entitled to.

Myles began to advance slightly with the special education class. There were intervals when three or four days would pass without even hearing his voice. It was scary. I concluded that the development of his brain was interrupted when I miscarried his twin. The bleeding must have affected his growth and development.

One day, I was alone at home. And my depression was overwhelming. I lay in my bed and cried. I wanted so much more for my children, for myself. I wanted a man that loved me, and wanted to spend time with me. I wanted a man that loved his kids and wanted to spend time with them. It always felt like being with us, being around us was a chore for Kennith. We would be opening Christmas presents, and I would have to pull him into the occasion. We would be at dinner in a restaurant, and he would be talking on his cell phone during the meal. My older kids started to complain to me about this time. Marcel would ask why we stayed in Alabama if Daddy was never home? And Shayna began to pull away from him even more.

I lay in the bed, crying and asking God to help me. I was angry with myself for staying with him. I was afraid to leave. I felt guilty for wanting to take his children and leave. I couldn't understand why my prayers weren't changing him. I didn't understand why Myles had to be Special. I began to worry about his future, and if I would be able to raise him.

I had never, ever considered suicide as an option. But, for a few seconds, I thought that death must be easier than the pain I was in. Suddenly, I felt a calm in my Spirit. It was a feeling I had never experienced in my life. I felt as if all was perfect in the world. It was a perfect peace. God spoke to me and told me that He could give me perfect peace. A very small twinkling of hope was gifted to me, and with it I realized that I had a mustard seed of faith hiding deep within my spirit.

I sought Counseling, and I clung to every Bible verse, Christian Television Show, I would go to Books A Million whenever I needed some space from K and the kids. At this time, Valeria was my only friend. And I got to a point where I could no longer speak about how I was feeling. I was tired of hearing myself complain about my husband and about my life. Once again, I felt like I was going to have an emotional breakdown. I called a Christian Counseling office that was near my home. I set up an appointment, and went in and spoke with a male counselor. I didn't tell anyone I was in counseling. Sometimes a young Mother and wife goes through seasons where it feels like nothing is about you. You feel like you can't even have a meal without an interruption, you can't go to the toilet without someone calling out for "Mommy", I felt like I had nothing. I felt like everything, including my kids were K's. They looked like him, even Marcel. It's stunning how much he and Myles looked alike. We lived around his family, in places that he knew and was familiar with. We visited his friends. We spent holidays with his family. We would run into people he knew at the grocery store. Everything was all about him. I was lost. I had lost sight of who I was, and I had no idea how to find me again.

One day, shortly after telling the kids about Kenny's other son., I told K "If you can't keep your dick to yourself, you need to have a vasectomy. You can't afford any more kids." And he did. We went to the appointment, scheduled it, and a cosmetic repair to his penis and he had a vasectomy. Afterwards we went home and I was the attentive wife. Part of me was relieved he couldn't make any more babies, and part of me felt like a damn fool. I was the attentive wife, helping my husband make sure he didn't get anyone else pregnant! Yes, I was a damned fool.

I was overwhelmingly lonely. As I began to talk to my counselor, I told him of the recent years events. What our family had gone through. I told him my goals were to find purpose for my life, apart from K. I told him that I felt like I was holding on for dear life, and that death would be better than this. We journeyed through my childhood and the fears and the violence that lived in those memories. I shared my feelings of resentment and loneliness, feeling both angry that my family did not make efforts to visit me, and then feeling guilty expecting them to.

He listened. He told me that I had expectations of myself that were not reachable. And he told me that my emotions were real, and that they were in line with my experiences. He told me that I was not crazy. He taught me that if I were to feel normal while going through that experience, that then I would be *"crazy."* I was able to share my fears. We talked about love, and what I thought that love was and meant. He helped me to see that loving Kenny was not my problem; allowing K to mistreat me was my problem. I had always thought I had such high self-esteem. I conclude that one can be just as damaged by high self-esteem as by low. I thought that if I was a good Mother and Wife that he would love me back. I hung on because I was good, and because I could not accept it if my marriage failed. I didn't ever ask myself, *"What am I doing wrong? Why doesn't he love me?"* I was more like, *"This man better love me, I'm good. And we are gonna be good together. And I am going to hold on until the good part comes."* It felt better just to talk about it. Slowly, I began to heal, very slowly. So slowly in fact that I am still healing.

Most importantly, I began to see that I had been abusive to my kids. I was strict, K and I both were. But, I was too quick to slap Marcel and Shayna. As my emotions came into better alignment I regretted my actions, and I vowed to only spank my kids when they needed it. I began to work on having individual relationships with each of my kids. I became a better Mother. My episodes of depression lessened in length and frequency. I talked with the kids, and encouraged them to share their feelings and tell me what they really thought about. I apologized to them and promised to be more loving and attentive. I was ashamed that I let my bad marriage allow me an excuse to hurt my kids.

The kids and I began to go to church at a large predominantly white church. The Pastor and staff were anointed, and the kids had plenty of activities to keep them involved in. I began to really learn about the Bible in a way I could apply to my life. K's Aunt, Gennetta, introduced me to the church. Eventually, I became a member. I would be baptized in the church several years later. K rarely visited church with us. Usually, it was the kids and me. We took the kids to Orlando for vacation that year. It was fun but exhausting, I just always was exhausted with being the one to plan and execute everything. Kenny and the kids looked to me for everything, so vacation didn't always feel like a vacation. And with all the arguments and stress in our lives, it was very difficult. I felt like we were pretending to be a family, and I was no longer able to put up a front.

Disney world, Orlando Florida 2006

Another Move

K wanted to move. He said it was because we live on the downside of a small hill and it was dangerous to pull in and out of the driveway and for the kids to play in the front yard. I agreed. We were just starting to have a little more financial peace. We searched and searched. I found a home in a nice subdivision of an area called Spanish Fort, in Spanish Fort Estates. It was an older house built in 1970, so it had larger rooms that the new homes we looked at. It had a two-car garage. I desperately wanted to be able to park in a garage. A large den, a large Master bedroom downstairs for us, another Master bedroom with full bath upstairs for Marcel, a large room for Shayna, a smaller room for KJ and Myles and a third full bath, there was also a half-bath downstairs for guests to use. The point that sold Kenny was an office off the den and garage that could be used for a studio. The home was empty, needed a little work, but we could afford it. I saw it as a place we could grow in. I imagined us living there, entertaining, and making home improvements. We put in an offer, and we bought a house.

Or so we thought. Two weeks after closing on the home, being given the keys and taking possession of the house, there was a knock on the door. A woman stood there and told me that we were not supposed to be in the house, the sale did not go through! I listened, took her information and called my Realtor. Thankfully, I did not call the usual number to reach her. I called 411 for the number, and when I called I reached our Agent's Broker. I told her what happened, I was in tears. Kenny came home, and we were both in shock. The next day, we met with our Agent, her Broker and owner of the Real Estate Company, and the other Agent. Our agent and broker agreed that they would fix the situation, without any cost to us. And they did. We did not have to sue anyone; our agent had to pay any costs above and beyond what was agreed to in the first contract. It was quite an experience. But, we had become accustomed to challenges, and this was one time where we pulled together and didn't attack one another under stress.

We moved in. I painted, and decorated. I started to feel some happiness again. I was busy, enrolling the kids in school and establishing our new home. I had always longed to do things together. I would be outside doing the yard, and K would be doing something else. If I wanted to wash the cars together, he would complain that I couldn't do things by myself. I did everything for myself. We rarely shopped together. I didn't go to his shows and events. I wasn't welcome in the studio. He was absent mentally even if he was present physically. I asked him to go to counseling with me. He didn't.

The kids and Lyte at a Show in Atlanta.

I started taking Celexa for depression after seeing my doctor and after discussing it with my counselor. I began to feel the clouds fading. I tried so many different approaches to K. I knew he was tired of hearing about the past, he told me so. I tried to move on, face the new day. I tried to be nicer, friendlier, and not complain. I tried to be Suzy homemaker; I tried to give him what he needed sexually. I stopped looking for signs of infidelity. He would probably say that I never stopped. But, I did. I prayed hard a long for my family. I asked him to come to church with us. I began to feel that God could heal us, and I believed he would.

I was still insecure and easily mistrusting of K. On my birthday, I told K all I wanted was to go spend the night somewhere, anywhere. Have one night's dinner, and one night with him away from the kids. I needed it. He went out of town the weekend of my birthday. He didn't leave a gift, a card. He didn't even take the kids to buy me a card. Shayna and Marcel still remember that I drove them to Dollar Tree, and gave them each $5.00, which was just about all I had, and I told them to go in the store and buy me gifts. They did, and then they went home and wrapped them. Marcel got me a white silk tulip in a glass vase, a card, and some candy. Shayna got me a shower sponge, and some shower gel, a card, and a candle. That night, I prayed and asked God to show K all of his wrongs.

God ended up showing me all of mines. He told me to leave Kennith to him. He told me to step out of the way, and he would work on Kennith. He told me that K was his son, just as I was his daughter and he told me that I was to get stronger, I was to increase my faith, that I needed to pray for Kennith and stop talking to Kennith, and that I needed to take my focus off of

Kenny and put my focus onto Him to get through what was coming. I was mad. "God, why do I always have to be the bigger person? Why do I have to be the one praying for him? Haven't I been through enough? I deserve my family! I deserve Kennith's love! I stood strong through all that came my way, and even when I thought I was, I DIDN'T BREAK!" I cried, like the crybaby I was born to be, and I tried to let go of my husband.

Me in our Spanish Fort home in the middle of my depression.

Shayna and Marcel laid on my bed one day. Apparently, they had been talking. Marcel told me that they wanted to call Dr. Phil to help our family. I listened. Shayna interjected with tears, "I don't know why we have to live here. We hate it here. And you keep telling us that family is the most important thing, and you keep trying to save your marriage. But, everybody knows Dad cheats on you. He doesn't care about us. Why can't we just leave and go to California?" It hurt to hear my kids tell me the truth. Marcel said that as soon as he graduated he was moving to California, he didn't care what he had to do. He said that he loved his Dad, but that Dad was never home, and was never a part of family things. I told them that we were a family, and that we would fight to stay together. I understood Marcel wanting to live in California, and it scared me, but I knew I couldn't stop him.

I asked Shayna what made them think their Dad was cheating on me, she said "Mom, we're not stupid, we have 2 brothers the same age. Dad is never home, and he never acts like he wants to be with us. He says he's working, but he tells us he never has any money. He buys stuff for the studio, then tells us he is broke."

I took our conversation to K. His response was that I was filling their heads with lies. He felt that I should have told them, and made them believe that he is away from home because he is working for his family, making money to provide. Then he said the kids needed to tell him, and not me, how they feel. The kids didn't have a relationship with him at that time. They had grown apart from him, just as he had grown apart from us. And they were afraid of him. Communication with K has always been difficult. I empathized with the kids and their inability to communicate with him.

Changes of Life

In June of 2007, I had a hysterectomy. I had waited long enough after my Doctor kept suggesting one, and I ended up anemic from the excess bleeding I experienced. My Mother doesn't travel, and she suggested my sister come and stay with me to help. My sister, Karla, nine years my senior, came to my home.

My sisters and I have times when we are very close and times when we can't stand each other. At this time, my sister was coming into her gifts of the Prophetic anointing. I sometimes, no a lot of times, felt that her Prophecies were more personal opinion than God given prophesy. At least where her family was concerned. The visit started off okay. By this time, I had shared some of my marriage woes with my family. And like any other family, they were concerned.

I had the surgery and K spent the first night with me. He had to go back to work so my sister spent the next night. About midnight, second day out of surgery, I began to violently and profusely vomit. I knew from the looks of the vomitus and my symptoms that I had a bowel blockage before the Doctors told me. I was given the necessary medications, a tube was placed down my nose and into my stomach to drain the stomach contents, and I couldn't eat. The medication helped me to sleep the rest of that night.

The next morning, my sister pulled a chair up to my bedside and commenced to tell me that my marriage was over, my kids were suffering because of our lifestyle, and our choices and that K was a terrible husband. I might have agreed with most of what she said. But, as they say, timing is everything. She would have been more effective at that time has she taken a warm cloth and put it on my forehead, prayed for me, loved on me. In the far future, I would be able to share with her what hurt me that day.

I would be well enough to go home in a few days, and I did. At home, I noticed that my sister had a major attitude with K. I understood, but I also felt that when you are in someone's home you should respect him or her. We tried to enjoy the rest of the visit.

I decided to take the kids and go to California for a few days, I had some money stashed, and K helped a little bit, so we flew to Cali. I needed it so bad. I missed my Mother terribly. We enjoyed ourselves. I spent time with my nieces and nephews; they were growing and coming into their own careers and relationships. I had a few great nieces and nephews I got to meet.

Shayna and I were driving down foothill Boulevard, when she opened up. "Mom, we are all miserable in Alabama. Why can't you just leave Dad? You are always by yourself anyway. He doesn't care about us." I stared ahead and told her. "I'm going to give your Dad one more year. If he doesn't become a better Father and Husband I will think about what to do then." I had been thinking years. I knew that KJ wouldn't want to leave. I didn't have the money, or the energy to fight him. He had his parent's money behind him, and nobody was behind me. I was afraid of being alone, of being even poorer, and not being able to provide for my kids. I prayed long and hard, and I asked God to show me what to do. I asked God to change Kennith. He had one year.

I was at my biggest. My neck and my abdomen felt swollen and full following my Hysterectomy. Poor self-esteem began to take a hold of me. The years trying to fight for my husband's attention, depression, and bitterness had my emotions in a whirlwind and the Hysterectomy had my hormones in an uproar. Hot flashes were the most uncomfortable part physically, but the upset to my self-esteem seemed to cut down into my spirit.   It was time for my twenty-year class reunion. Kenny and I went, it was the one of the only times we took a vacation without kids since I had moved to New York.

Kenny and I at my 20-year reunion in California in 2007.

In My Bed

Kennith asked me to go to a show with him. That was very unlike him and it made me feel good. The show was in Birmingham. We had a good time. We spent the weekend and enjoyed ourselves. It was rare for us. I tried to ignore all the signs flashing in my face that he was still a cheater. At that point, I didn't take it personal. I thought he had some kind of an addiction. There was no way he could have an emotional attachment to these women, it was mathematically and physical impossible. He was going for quantity and not quality. I tried to ignore it, because God had told me not to focus on Kennith. But, it built up in my system and I felt like I would implode inside.

Birmingham, Alabama 2007

MySpace was big then. And I wondered why K didn't have his family on his page. Then he put us on it, and I felt good. I only had a few friends on there, mostly from California and it was fun getting back in touch with old friends. The kids were on it, and it was a nice distraction from life.

One day, I noticed the name on Kenny's phone. She was a frequent caller. He had changed phones, and something told me to charge and look through his old one. I found pictures of a female. I did a little research, and found that she was a friend with one of my friends on MySpace. I didn't know the girl who was listed as my friend, I had only added her because she was in a nurse and I figured that she was someone I had known or met briefly at the hospital. As I looked through the photos, I saw that Kennith was having a relationship with this woman. I was disgusted that her friend was on my page, and realized the two women were spying on me. I sent each a brief note by way of MySpace, telling them that they were scandalous, and that I knew she was sleeping with my husband.

KJ had played football and had attended school with a young boy, and I had become acquainted with his mother. His young Mother also worked at one of the Nursing Homes where I Case-Managed some Hospice patients. Each day I struggled with the thought of leaving Kennith. I struggled knowing that KJ would not want to leave Alabama. I struggled knowing that if I left this would be the last time. Every scenario swam through my head every moment of the day. I went through all the motions of life, weighing the decision of my family's future every second of the day.

I sat in a small room charting when the young woman came in and said hello. We chit chatted for a few moments, mostly talking about her Baby Girl that she had given birth to a few months earlier. When she told me that she was looking for a house in the subdivision I lived in, I asked her why? She lived in one of the nicer subdivisions in a beautiful home, and I couldn't see her wanting to move.

"I'm getting a divorce. It's almost final, we sold the house and I have to downsize." She told me. She must have seen the shock on my face, I thought they were a happy family. They were always at the games together and at school functions, and their baby girl was only a few months old. She continued, "He came home one day and told me that he was in love with someone else. He had been having an affair with her for years, and I never knew a thing." My heart fluttered, "Oh My God." Was all that I could say. "Yeah, he said that he couldn't stand being away from her and we're done."

I was jealous. I was jealous because she was free. And I was still a captive of lies. I wished my husband had the strength to tell me the truth and to set me free. I knew Kennith wouldn't ever set me free. I knew that I would have to fight for my freedom. And it would be the hardest fight of my life.

In March of 2008, I told K I wanted a divorce. I told him I was leaving him. He told me he would fight for the kids to stay in Alabama. We fought back and forth for about two weeks. Marcel's graduation day came. He had told me for years that as soon as he graduated he would be moving back to California. I knew I would miss my son, but I fully understood why he wanted to leave. Our family was the reason I always gave my kids for not living in California. At that point, there was no sense in using that as an argument for Marcel to stay. Our family was falling apart, and we all knew it.

Making things even harder, we became God-Parents to

Haile. One of Kenny's cousin's daughters. I loved her so much.

Shayna and I spent a lot of time with her and I was disappointed

that I wouldn't be around to be with her as she grew up.

Marcel's Graduation Day from Spanish Fort High School.

"So, I hear you are moving. I wouldn't take that bed,

because OOPS, I made a mess in it. Remember when you were in

California, after your surgery..." I don't remember the rest, but

she told me she was in my house, and IN MY BED! That was

what she wrote on Myspace. And to make matters worse, my

daughter saw it. She had been watching her Dad's Myspace page

for a while, and she was suspect of the girl before I was. That was deep; I had to show my daughter that we do not have to take that kind of disrespect. I had to stand up for myself and for my kids. I made an appointment with my Pastor. I told him my story, and I asked if God would allow me a Divorce. Kennith didn't protect me; he told me it was my fault for contacting her in the first place. Never mind, that her friend had conned me into adding her, so they were watching me for months. I talked to the kids. KJ wanted to stay. He was the only one. Myles was only I told Kenny I wanted a Divorce, for real. I made an appointment to see an attorney. I tried to talk to Kenny about the details, like visitation, how to split up the home, and he talked back, sometimes. I slept upstairs in Marcel's room. He had graduated and was already in California.

The day of the appointment, I was driving to the lawyer's office when Kennith called me. He asked where I was, and I told him I was on my way to see a lawyer. He got mad, said we were supposed to go together. I didn't care, I went to the appointment, and I gave her my info and pain my retainer. As in the past, we would file taxes together, and then K would want to split to refund. He would spend his on whatever, and I would pay for a vacation and buy the kids what they needed. This year he had his half and I spent my half on my lawyer.

When I went home K was in his studio. I wanted to speak to him about what the lawyer and I discussed. After all, we were trying to amicable. He went off. He told me I wasn't taking his kids, he wasn't paying any child support, he wasn't giving me my portion of his retirement, and I had no right to HIS house. He told me everything was HIS. I became so irate, that I had to leave. I got in my car and I drove. I drove a short distance and pulled over and sat on a small beach at the gulf. I cried out to God. And He answered. He told me that HE was my Provider and if Kennith wanted all of it, then GIVE it to Him. And I would see just how My God Loved Me.

I went home and knocked on the door of the studio. Kennith wouldn't open it. He said through the door, "Naw, you are crazy, and you might want to shoot me or something. How you come back all calm?" I told him through the door, "If you really feel that I don't deserve anything. You can have it. You can have it all, just let me have my kids." And I went to my Lawyer the next day and told her that I didn't want to fight him for anything, but my kids. If any of them wanted to stay, they could stay. And that was that. On my drive home, I received a call. I had posted my resume on a website to see what kind of offers I could receive from California. I had never even heard of Hospice Nurses Travel Assignment, most Travel Nurses were Medical Surgical, or Hospital Specialty Nurses. The call was an offer for a Six-month assignment, near where my family lived, with an excellent rate of pay, and my choice of an apartment or a $2100 stipend for housing. When I calculated my portion of Kennith's Pension, and my portion of the small amount of equity we had in the home, it equaled about the same as 6 months of the living stipend. God was at work, and I knew it. My faith was weak, and my worries were huge, but, God kept me from drowning.

The divorce settlement stated that I would get the furnishings of the house, my Ford Explorer, and Shayna and Myles would go to California with me. He got the house, His

Suburban, the truck Reggie had left him, an old Cadillac we had, all of his retirement, he did not have to pay me any child support or spousal support, and KJ wanted to remain with his Father. Kennith would hide any income he earned from the Studio or DJ'ing, none of it was included in the divorce paperwork, and I did not argue. I just wanted to finally be free from his lies, his cheating, and his disrespect. I didn't care the cost. Leaving KJ would break my heart. But, I knew boys needed their Dads. I knew that KJ had a good relationship with Kennith's parents, and the schools were excellent in the area. I trusted that Kennith would provide the necessities for KJ, but, I worried that Kennith would not provide the spiritual and emotional support for him. I did not want to leave my son, but I felt that I had no choice. I was not healthy in Alabama, and I knew it. I had to fix whatever was wrong with me, and unfortunately that meant my son would be staying in Alabama.

KJ's Birthday in the house in Spanish Fort.

One day I went to Kenny's parents' house, and Jesse and I sat in the den and talked about my leaving. He expressed how he wished we could try and make it work. Crying like always, I tried my best to express my hurt to him. I had tried everything to make my marriage work. And it was changing me for the worse. I needed to be free, and I needed to get away before something worse happened. I tried to explain my feelings to Jesse. Jesse was the only Father figure I had, and I thought that he had come to love me like a daughter. I asked him, "What would you tell me to do if I were your daughter by blood? Would you encourage me to stay and put up with all that Kenny has done if I were your daughter and he weren't your son?" Jesse didn't have an answer, and that hurt. I realized then that I was not loved like a daughter. As I got up to leave, I told him "You know, I am somebody's daughter, too. And they want to see me happy just like you want to see your daughter happy."

I had to leave. If I didn't one of us would have been in jail, and one of us very likely could have been dead. Kenny had pushed me beyond my limit. He had played with my love and with my family. I had been on so many ups with Kennith, and too many lows. I was no longer willing to die for him. Had he loved me back I would have continued to ride for him. But, I felt my very life draining out of me. And I wanted to live. I wanted peace of mind.

July 4th, 2008 was the last Holiday I planned to spend with Kenny's family. He wasn't there. He was out of town. The family didn't seem to believe that we were leaving. No one knew what was going on, they knew we were getting a divorce, but they didn't know why. I didn't tell anyone about Kenny's lies. I didn't want it to matter anymore. I was tired of feeling like a fool. I was tired of having to explain Kennith's wrongs. I felt that if they were really concerned they would talk to Kenny. I didn't want to tell them about Kenny and his affair. I just wanted to say Goodbye.

We remained in the house as I packed, planned on how to make the move. One weekend about 3 weeks before we were scheduled to leave, Kennith was going out of town. I decided to sell some furniture. It would make the trip easier, and since he had told me he would not be helping me drive to California, I needed as little baggage as possible. He left On Friday, and Shayna and I put up yard sale signs on Friday afternoon. Myles and KJ were with Kennith's parents. The next morning, we sold most of the household furnishings, including that damn bed that his mistress claimed to have slept in. I was leaving KJ's furniture of course, all the kitchenware, bathroom supplies, and the furniture in the den. KJ was staying and I wouldn't have him without anything. I was blessed. A lady came, and I recognized her from church. I loved my dining table, and hated to have to sell it. I sold it to her for $250.00, after she cried and told me she had never owned a dining table in her life and she was around

50 years old. I saw God everywhere I turned those weeks. I was

amazed at how God was present, even amongst the pain and the

strife of what I was going through.

Our Last Christmas as a Family 2007

Momma Got This

On July 7th, 2008, around 6am I backed my Black Ford

Explorer out of the driveway, Kennith kissed his kid's goodbye

and we were on our way to California. I had driven the road

several times, but never alone. I had it all mapped out. My kids were trained to take long road trips, Myles was only 6, and with his delays the kids already knew how to hurry and take him to the bathroom, to look out for each other, and to make sure he was okay. It surprised and disappointed me that Kennith even allowed me to drive so far alone with the kids. It was just one more disappointment piled atop all the others.

Shayna, KJ and Myles were good on the trip. I would only let myself cry when they were sleeping. Mary J Blige, Alicia Keys, Keyshia Cole, and Jennifer Hudson were my co-pilots. Urging me on, encouraging me to be strong. They sang what my heart felt, and my soul cried out. When I needed spiritual uplifting, it was Smokie Norful's "I Need You Now." That invited the Holy Spirit to comfort me. We stopped in Texas, just before nightfall to rest. I took the kids swimming in the indoor pool, and we ate room service. The next morning it was Hotel Breakfast, gas up and back on the road. The next stop was in New Mexico. It was still daylight, but I was tired, and we needed a break. I rented games in the room for the boys. Shayna told me that she would never forgive her Dad for not driving with us. She said that was proof that he did not care. I cried in the shower. My kids had seen enough of me crying, and putting up with abuse. I had to be stronger. I had to show them how strong the God in me was.

We drove all day. Shayna and I became more anxious as we began to navigate the twists and turns of entering California. The rocks along the way were familiar to us. And we cheered when we saw the fans. The tall white fans that signaled to us that we were almost home. We were going to stay with one of my nieces, Tiffany, and her fiancé when we arrived. I would start looking for an apartment soon. I was afraid, because I had filed Bankruptcy the last March also, and because I was legally still married I had to file Chapter 13 instead of the Clean Sweep Chapter 7. I didn't think I could find a place for my kids, and that worried me immensely. I should have relied on God, all that he showed me and I still worried about how I would provide. Forgetting that He would.

We arrived at Tiffany's house and unpacked some of our things. I held my Great-Nephew for the first time. Appreciating that I would get to know my family better now. I focused on the future, instead of the past. The yearning for Kennith's love and affection always a reminder of what I would never have. I was mad at myself for still loving him. I felt stupid for loving him. And I prayed to stop loving him.

A week later, my sister, Karla, called me and asked if we wanted to rent their Condo. Her stepdaughter owned it, and managed it. It was expensive, but being afraid that no one else would rent to me, I accepted. It was really nice. Two-car garage, two stories, in Rancho Cucamonga. We moved in and slept on the floor. We didn't have a TV, we didn't have anything. We borrowed an air mattress, and I started working. It was hard. I thought I was making good money, but starting from scratch cost a lot with three kids. KJ would be going back to his Dad at the end of the summer, but I had to provide for three kids immediately. Slowly but surely, I was able to get what we needed.

Two of my nieces ended up staying with us. Tiffany left her boyfriend, and Shannon came to stay. They paid a little rent, which helped. And I loved the company. I sometimes had to work at night, and it helped to have somebody there with the kids. Besides, I was trying to make up for lost time. I still cried a lot. Especially when my air mattress went flat. It hurt me to know that after all we had been through together Kennith didn't care. For the first six months I worked, slept, and grinded to get my kids what they needed. Most of my old friends didn't even know I had returned to California. I was weighting 220 pounds, and I was free.

By Christmas, I had furniture. And, thank God, I had a real bed. Things were coming together. KJ came back to visit. We took a lot of pictures. Every year, since the kids were small, I would send out Christmas Cards with pictures of the kids. People loved them. And this year, I raced to get out pictures out. I had lost some weight, and after yelling at the kids we got some nice shots. When I picked the pictures up from the drugstore, I noticed that I looked happier. I was starting to allow myself to live. The separation was getting easier. The divorce had become final in November.

In December, I fell apart. Kennith announced on MySpace that he was engaged, to his mistress. The girl who said she had slept in my bed. I was Heartbroken. How could he? He said he didn't want to be married, but he just didn't want to be married to me! I tried to keep going. I stayed in my room and cried. Marcel came over, and as soon as I looked at him I fell apart. He just held me on the stairs and told me "It's okay, Mom. You're going to be okay."

He moved her into my house less than 6 moths after I left. She was living there with my son. Her daughter was sleeping in my daughter's room. And he let me and my kids sleep on floors for months. I wanted to hate him. I tried to turn all the disappointments into hate. And it felt like hate. Shayna stopped speaking to him. The kids withdrew from him. I told them he had a right to move on. Shayna said she would not visit with that woman in the house. Kennith acted as if what he did was right. He hadn't told his kids he was getting married. I saw pictures of Kennith and her, with KJ on MySpace. I didn't know what to do with those feelings, all I knew was pain.

Shayna and I had gone to counseling; I wanted to help her with her feelings. She was growing to hate her Dad, and I didn't want that. He said I poisoned her against him. He barely called, didn't write. Barely sent any gifts or help. And I was poisoning them against him. I had to make her call him, and her Grandparents. They didn't call or write or send anything either. It was like out of sight out of mind. Meanwhile, KJ would call and brag that they bought him this, and they bought him that. They would say they didn't call because the kids were supposed to call them and Shayna had an attitude. But, why didn't they call Myles? What did he do? He wasn't able to call himself. I forced my kids to call their Dad and Grandparents, anyway. No one could have ever prepared me for the pain of those months. It took all I had to focus on starting a new life and making a home for my kids.

My family celebrated Christmas Eve at my house. It was the first time all four of my sisters had taken a picture with my Mother in years. All my nieces and nephews came. That helped me to carry on. I needed my family to get through this.

I would still miss Kennith, but he was moving on and so I needed to move on, too. KJ came for Christmas, and that was the last Christmas that we took our customary Holiday photos.

Christmas in Rancho Cucamonga, California 2008

My temporary employment ended in December of 2008, and I found a full-time job as a Hospice Case Manager. I was excited to have a full-time job. On my fifth day of employment, while orientating with another nurse, we were in a terrible accident on the 10 Freeway. I was a passenger. We were traveling about 60 Westbound on the Freeway, when a passenger truck lost control as they entered from the 215 North Onramp. The truck came skidding across the freeway and our car struck the truck at the driver's door, another car hit us from behind and we lost control. I remember screaming "JESUS! JESUS! JESUS!" over and over. I was wide awake as we spun and kept thinking that one of the other cars speeding on the freeway was going to hit us. We stopped and were facing oncoming traffic, and I saw that all the cars on the freeway were stopped, and people were running towards us. The Nurse driving was bleeding from the head, and my neck and left shoulder ached. All I could think was, "How am I going to take care of my kids now?"

At work on my travel nurse position, in
Whittier, California in October 2008.

One of the rudest Female CHP officers I ever met came to

the car. She lacked empathy, emotion, and was just plain rude.

She told me I didn't need an ambulance; I wasn't bleeding as my

co-worker was. I insisted. When we arrived at the hospital, and

the registration person came and told us she would have

Workman's Comp papers to fill out, I was relieved. I hadn't

thought of this being workman's Comp. I called my son, who left

school and came to the hospital. And I called my oldest sister,

Wanda, who came and prayed with us. My boss came, and

stayed briefly. That always surprised me. I knew that had I worked for Covenant Hospice, my boss and co-workers would have been more supportive.

I was released that night, and went home. My neck and back and my whole left side hurt so badly. My face even started to hurt. I remember calling for my daughter and she didn't hear me, I called and called, and by the time she heard me I was in tears. I was miserable for months after that accident. To top it all off, I would have no benefits since I was not actively working and was still on probation. I would only be making 2/3 of my pay, and I would be without health insurance, or any other benefit. There was a 14-day wait, and then compensation started. Once again, I fell into a financial hole. I asked Kennith for help, I asked him for money for groceries until my check came, and he sent nothing.

I became unable to pay my rent. I told my sister and my step-niece that I needed to move, because I would not be able to pay rent. My niece kept the security deposit and I owed a months rent. I felt bad, I didn't want to not pay, but I had to find a place for my kids to live. I prayed, and I went to an apartment complex in the area. I completed an application, and it was accepted. My kids and I moved into a two-bedroom apartment. I was relieved, but owing my niece would be both a humiliating and a guilt-ridden experience. I was told that if I were renting from anyone other than family, I would be expected to pay more due to breaking the lease. And I felt that I could have fought an eviction and got a couple months free rent if I had been renting from anyone other than family. This would be a very uncomfortable experience. I had to do what I had to do to put a roof over my kid's heads. My diabetes got out of control because I couldn't afford medications and I couldn't afford to see a doctor. Society thinks that people who don't have insurance have done something wrong. I had always had insurance, had worked, and was employed and found myself un-insured.

I was so angry with Kennith for not being there for the kids and me. Shayna tried out for Cheerleading, and I told her to call her Dad and tell him the good news. She called, and told him she made the team, and that it would cost over a thousand dollars. His response was "I don't know where you are going to get that from." Shayna was in tears, mad at me because I had made her call him. I told my daughter that I would do whatever to see that she was able to be on the team. I knew my money situation would be improving. Then all of a sudden, no workman's comp checks. It was mailed, but I didn't receive it. Rent was due in five days. Once again, I turned to Kennith. Once again, I was disappointed. My friend Monique from New York loaned me 100, and then told me not to pay her back, my Aunt Gennetta from Alabama loaned me $600 and only had me pay her back $400, Marqueta, a friend from Alabama loaned me $125. And I pawned my truck title for the rest, and to pay bills and buy groceries. Lord help anybody that EVER had to pawn a title. That is a complete rip off. I pray that somebody put a stop to that scam now.

Social Media

Needing a sense of security, I reached out to D, again. Being around him always made me feel safe. We spent time together, but, the very first time we slept together I knew that old feeling was gone. I began to see my tendency to hold onto my fantasies. He wasn't my long-lost soul-mate, he was a man who I had once cared about, and who was now a very dear friend. We tried for a minute to see what would happen. Eventually, we both recognized that our window for being a couple has past or was never there to begin with.

At the urging of my friend, I signed up on FaceBook. And I came into contact with people I hadn't seen in many years. It felt good to hear from people who knew the old me, the confident me, the me who would have never let a man destroy my self-respect. I had always been popular in school, and new many people. I needed some friends, some companionship. After speaking with several people from High School, I planned somewhat of a reunion. I planned for a bunch of us to meet at BJ's a nice eatery in the area. About thirty people showed up, and to my surprise, some who didn't even attend Garey High School, but had attended other High School in my hometown of Pomona. We had a good time. Our circle of contacts on FaceBook kept growing. Those who missed it, asked for more. I began to plan outings and get together for the Alumni from my High School. I teamed up with some Promoters for the area who I knew back in the day, and gave a party at a local club. We had a great turn out and a lot of fun.

Picture of me at one of my Garey High Alumni Functions in May 2009.

This would be the night that I would meet, or rather be re-introduced to R. R caught my eye because his whole character was just different. He had contacted me a few times on FaceBook, but so had many other men who flirted with me. Many who had stories of how they had watched me, admired me, or had a crush on me in High School or even Junior High. It was flattering. It helped me to remember the me who hadn't been cheated on and abused. I began to remember how I was before I had kids and before I lost myself in my marriage. I reconnected with some good friends who I had barely kept in contact over the years.

I flirted with R, and he flirted back. We exchanged numbers, and it would be a week or two before we would talk. We actually were supposed to go to breakfast after the club, but there were miscommunications and we didn't. We spoke on the phone, and by FaceBook and he would come to California three weeks later to take me out.   He was staying at the Doubletree Inn, and I was supposed to drive there and meet him. We didn't have concrete plans, I just wanted to be out, and I wanted to laugh, and talk and just enjoy myself.   I stopped by a liquor store on the way and picked up some drink. When I arrived at the Hotel, I went in and he met me in the hallway. I sat in a chair in the room while he finished getting dressed. He was clean, sMarcelled good, and dressed well. He is into his clothes, and had good taste in fashion. He shares with me that he used to own a clothing store, had spent time in jail, but had been out and working for eight years. He had no children, and was not married. Unfortunately, he was in a relationship.

I went out with him anyway. Craving attention, I didn't think about the consequences. Things were comfortable with him, he was like home. He had grown up on the South Side of Pomona, too. We knew the same people, places, our experiences were different. He was the type of man I was running from all those years ago when I was eager to move to New York. We got on the 10 Freeway and headed for Los Angeles. Roscoe's Chicken and Waffles was our dinner for the night. We talked and laughed. He told me that he wanted to make me feel young again. He was four years younger than me. A Freshman when I was a Senior. He, too, had his story of watching Rayna Bias and hoping to have a woman like her one day. I found it funny, wondering if he and the others would still want me knowing all that I had been through. Here I was, starting over, with four kids, and not much to show for the last twenty years of my life. I had left all my work in Alabama. The only good things I had to show for my life were my four kids, and my Nursing license.

My sisters and I January of 2010, still not
completely reconciled we all managed to show
up for my eldest sister's Birthday Party.

We continued to date for the next two years. He would
visit me and I would visit him. He was in a relationship, but he
cared about me. And I knew it. It would be two months later
that I would meet C. C and I met through my niece, and we spent
the night together the first night we met. I can thank Patron
Silver for that. We would continue to spend time, or rather, have

sex together for the next two years, also. So here I was, two men and still incomplete. Doing things just for the sake of doing them, all along wishing I were somebody's wife. I didn't spend a lot of time with either man. I would meet other men in between, none of which really made a deep impression on me. I began to have a very active social life, planning parties and outings with my friends, promoting parties for my homeboys, going to local bars and restaurants. And I was working on starting a Charity to benefit my hometown of Pomona with a girlfriend of mine.

I was becoming more and more angry at Kennith's lack of involvement with his children. When I would ask for help, Kennith would respond, "If you can't take care of my kids, send them to me." He would barely help financially. The Summer of 2009 came, and I was so frustrated. KJ came to visit, and He and Myles would fly back to Alabama. I was so tired of Kennith's lack of financial support that I agreed to let Myles live with him for a year. I was also very displeased with the Special Education System in California. Myles was lost in the system. He wasn't progressing, and he missed his Dad. I was feeling like a failure, things were not going as I planned, I was in pain, and I was frustrated.

I trusted Kennith to take good care of my kids. I trusted that even though I didn't like his girlfriend, I trusted that he would make sure his kids were taken care of. I was also trying to be fair, and to not keep Kennith's kids from his because of who he chose to be with. I missed my kids, and I thought that I would be able to spend more time with Shayna. Shayna had pulled all the way away. She didn't want to spend time with me. She was into her friends, and into boys. I knew she needed her Dad's attention. She resented him, and his parents. She felt like they had abandoned her because she chose to stay with me. She was angry, and I didn't know what to do about it. We went to counseling, she opened up, but it didn't seem to be helping to heal her pain. I gave her space. We would fight, and argue. She kept busy with Cheerleading and Dance. Marcel was working, living with my Mother. He lived with us for a short time, but we didn't agree on some things and he had to move. I love my kids, but I refuse to allow them to risk my home. We had already slept on floors, and I was not going to let anybody take us back there. I felt like anyone, including my kids was either on my team or sitting on the sidelines. Either way, I was in the game.

Myles seemed happy. We would talk on the phone, and I would send them things. I prayed that they were being treated well. I was confident that Kennith's large family would look out for them. They were Moorer's and I thought that they would not let anything happen to them. Kennith and I only talked about the kids and nothing more. We were both moving on with our lives. It angered me that I had to let my boys be there in order to get any help from him, but I also appreciated the break. I was exhausted, completely. I never felt whole. When my kids are not in my reach I long for them. The motions of life continue, but the sun is not as bright, and the air not as clear until they are with me again.

October of 2009, Kennith texted me and asked me how much plane tickets cost from LA to Hawaii. He told me that he would be spending a few days in Hawaii to DJ with Lyte. I figured that he wanted Shayna and Marcel to meet him there.

No, he wanted me to meet him there. It made no sense. I didn't go. We texted back and forth a while, and that started us talking sometimes. He told me that he missed me, and he wished he could do something nice for me. I was still stupid in love with Kennith. And I was feeling bolder, especially having other men in my life. Kennith asked for pictures, sexy pictures. And I sent them. They were cute and sexy. He wasn't the only man I sent them to, though. Part of me was getting revenge, she had messed with my man, and now I was messing with who she thought was her man. I found out around that Christmas that they had gotten married. This new only caused me to cry for three days, I was getting better. He hadn't told the kids he was married. Once again, they were hurt and expressed all the reasons he gave them to prove he didn't care about them.

I had an opportunity to chat with Lyte at the end of 2009. She invited Shayna and two of her friends out to LA. I drove them there, and had a brief moment to speak with her. I asked her if she could intervene between Shayna and Kennith. I didn't go into detail, but I told her that Shayna was having a real hard time with her Dad, and didn't want to contact him. I guess I expected her to sympathize with Shayna, knowing the void that a failed Father-Daughter Relationship can leave inside a young girl. We had never spoken about any problems Kenny and I had. I figured that she saw some of the other women coming and going. At that point, I thought everyone was aware of Kennith's shenanigans and understood exactly why I left.

Her response to me was "You should work on forgiving him and not being angry." At the time, I was angry and frustrated that yet again, I was being told that I was the problem. When was somebody going to understand that my kids were hurting? When was somebody going to understand that Kennith was wrong, what he did to me was wrong? What he did to our children was wrong. And what he did to our family was wrong. I expected Lyte, for some unknown reason to understand my plight. I left that day wanting to enjoy my freedom, that is the day that it first occurred to me that I may never get answers. It occurred to me that nobody may never understand the pain I felt. I had to go on. I had to stop searching for someone to grasp the tragedy of my broken family. I decided that day to be just a little bit happier, and to grab on to my Happy and never let go. The girls and I went to Venice Beach and had fun, we made crazy videos and my laugh was just deeper than I had remembered it being in a long time.

I was not going to have my boys on Christmas, and I missed them terribly. Kennith hardly ever complied with the court order to buy the kids airline tickets for their visitation with me. I longed to have a Christmas Photo of my kids together as I had done every year since Shayna and Marcel were little. It felt like I had to let go of everything, Kennith always won. And I always had to find a way to forgive and to let go. Christmas was not the same that year, and I posted a status on FaceBook saying that all I wanted for Christmas was for my kids to be together and for us to take our annual Christmas Photo. Christmas came without Shayna and Marcel receiving a gift or any acknowledgement from Kenny. It was my first Christmas ever without my kids.

A few days after New Year's, I received a Photo Card in the mail. It had pictures of KJ, Myles and his mistress' daughter and it said Happy New Year from the Moorers. It hit a sore spot. It hit a few sore spots. I was angry. So, she had my address to send me a Card, but she didn't think to make sure Shayna had a Christmas Present? And all I wanted that year was a Christmas Photo of all my children. I wrote her a letter on MySpace, I told her that she had no business sending me anything. If she wanted to send something so bad, it should have been a present for Shayna and Marcel. I also informed her of Kennith's invitation to take me to Hawaii. I had no idea he was married when he invited me.

Around January 24th, 2010 KJ told me that he had been sick and missed school. I questioned him, asking him if his Dad took him to Dr. Johnson. KJ said no, he said that he went to work with her. I asked him if she took him there to see a doctor, knowing that she worked at the County Health Department. He said, "No, I just went with her because I couldn't go to school." I asked him if he had any medicine, and he said, "She gave me a shot." I asked, "Gave you a shot where?" I was asking where I

his body, I was thinking that she had taken to the Health

Department Doctor and KJ just wasn't used to seeing that Doctor.

KJ responded, "She gave me a shot in the kitchen." "IN THE

KITCHEN? At home?" I asked. "Yes." He told me. "Was your

Dad home?" I asked, and KJ told me "No, but he knows she gave it

to me." I asked him where she gave him the shot on his body,

and he showed me his buttock. I called Kennith and asked him

what happened. Kennith told me that KJ had a fever and she,

who was an LVN, had given him an antibiotic shot. I asked, "Did

she give Myles a shot?" Kennith denied Myles being given a shot,

but, to this day I believe she did.

I was irate. I cussed Kenny out. I couldn't understand

why KJ wasn't taken to the Pediatrician I had taken them to the

entire time we lived in Alabama. My kids have Blue Cross/Blue

Shield, why would KJ be given a shot of who knows what in the

kitchen by an LVN? "I'm an RN, and I have NEVER given my kids

a shot! I take them to their doctor! What was in the shot? Why

the hell would you allow that? Do you understand the reason

shots are recorded? What if he is allergic? You don't know if she gave him something harmful! I don't trust that Bitch!" My rant was met with a dial tone. "Damn!" I threw the phone at the wall, and I fell to my knees. I was in a daze, my prayer language mixed with tears, moans, and grunts. "God, please. Please. Please. Protect my children."

January 26th, 2010 at 5:30 am, Kennith's cell phone number glared across the screen of my cell phone. He was crying, and told me that Myles was being rushed to the Emergency Room by ambulance. Myles had a Seizure. I felt to my knees and called on my God, my prayer language flowed freely from my lips as I begged God to save my child and get me to him. I was able to board a plane that morning; I arrived in Alabama that evening. Myles had been released from the hospital, but a Seizure? No one in our family had seizures. And being a nurse, I had witnessed plenty. I knew all of the things that a seizure could indicate and I needed to be with my son. My friend Val and her sister picked me up from the airport. She drove me to Aunt Gennetta's house; K was to meet me there with my boys. I held both my sons. Gennetta had lost her Mother that week, and it was a blessing to be able to be there for her at the same time as be there for my son.

Myles was scheduled for tests the following day. I spent the next night with my friend, Val, and took Myles to the hospital for an EEG the next morning. While sitting in the waiting room, Kennith walked in. I was surprised because the plan was for me to take him and for Kennith to go to work. It was the first time we had been in the same room in years. The circumstances kept me focused on Myles, and I was proud of myself for being able to keep Kenny out of my emotions. After the test, we went to eat at the new Five Guys. Kenny couldn't afford lunch, and I bought us all lunch. It was a kind of justice. He had taken so much from me, and I was not only able emotionally, but able financially to by him lunch. The irony made me feel a little bit stronger.

The plan was for Kennith to bring KJ to Val's house after school. When Kenny came to drop KJ off, Kenny asked me to come outside to talk. Kennith told me that his new wife was trippin'. He said that she had insisted on riding with him to my friend's house to drop off KJ, and when he told her "No." She had acted a fool, even trying to follow him over the bridge. He said she was accusing us of having an affair. I laughed. So, she didn't like her own medicine? I brought up the shot, and Kennith admitted he was wrong. Why would you NOT take my sick son to the same doctor he has had for years, the kids have insurance, why would you let her give my son a shot. I explained the many ways that she was wrong, and I told Kennith that I was reporting her. He didn't disagree.

Can't Walk in My Shoes

Val and I were sitting outside of Dollar General, when Shayna called my cell. "Who is N*** Hall?" Shayna asked. "Your Dad's Wife" was my response. "Well, she's rude. She hung up in my face." Shayna told me. "What, when, what happened? How do you know it was her?" I asked. "Caller ID. She called and said 'Can I speak to Rayna? I told her you weren't here and she hung up in my face." Shayna said. Shayna gave me the number for NH, and I hung up.

I called NH. "This is Rayna, you looking for me?" I asked. She had an attitude, "Yes, you playing with my Husband." I laughed, "I been here for 3 days, and you think I am fucking Kennith. Oh, so now the shoe is on the other foot, huh? And you can't handle it? I know, he leaving you at home with the kids now, huh? It was okay when it was me, but now you mad? You can't fill my shoes, "Bitch. I gave you a man, a house, and some kids, and you losing your Fucking mind. " she yelled and screamed all kinds of obscenities.

"And I should fuck you up for giving my son a shot. Trust and believe, you will get yours." And she hung up. I immediately called Kennith and told him what happened. Kennith commenced to tell me "That bitch is leaving my house. Fuck her; you should go fuck her up. That crazy bitch." Val laughed, she could hear him. I wanted to kick her ass with everything inside of me. I told him he better go and check her for being rude to my daughter

Grandma's Porch

I was so angry that this woman seemed to be living my life. And I was even angrier that she got to have My Grandma. Lee Ella Moorer was Kennith's Paternal Grandmother. She was MY GRANDMOTHER. I respected her, I loved her, and I missed her. She loved me, and she liked me. When I lived in Alabama, I got tired of sitting on Grandma's Porch. When I was in California, I longed for it. I missed her voice, her hands, her hugs, her prayers, and her being the Matriarch of our family. Yes, I was very jealous that NH was welcomed into what should have been my family. I didn't like thinking that she was receiving the blessings of my Grandmother.

My Grandmother hugged me, and held my hands. She was happy to see me. Kennith came to the funeral with his parents; no wife. I thought that was strange. I was sure she wanted to go, but then again, it didn't matter.   At the repast, Grandma and I talked. She prayed for Myles, laying hands on him. And she told me these words, "Get your kids out of that house, that girl ain't right." I told her that I didn't think Kennith would let me, she told me "Those kids need to be with you, I don't trust her."   Grandma had already heard about the shot incident, and she told me playfully, "I will hold her down while you beat her."

My Grandma, Lee Ella Moorer, and I
in 2011.

I missed the family dinners, the holidays, and the visits. I
felt like I hadn't had a chance to get close to the family because I
was always paranoid and mad at Kennith. I wished I had an
opportunity for them to know the real me, not the insecure me.

I had also felt very betrayed by his family. Looking from
where I stood, it seemed that the family had been okay with the
way Kennith had treated me. His cousins seemed to be close to

his new wife, and that hurt. When I left, I didn't tell everyone that he was having an affair. I didn't tell them her name, or that she said she had slept in my bed. But, didn't it seem strange that she came around just a few months after I left? Did anybody ask Kenny what was that about? One of his cousins in particular, had really hurt my feelings. I did tell the family about the shot she gave KJ, and though most of them did not approve. No one stepped up for my kids. It hurt because I thought they would have all looked out for my kids better than they had. And I was mad at myself for believing Kennith would have done a better job of looking out for them.

That night, I got one more call from NH Hall, she called my phone and yelled, "Keep Your Damn Kids Away from my house!" and I yelled back "Bitch, ARE YOU THREATENING MY KIDS?" and her reply was "WATCH!" I called Kennith hysterical, he said he had just left and that they had been fighting. I told him she threatened my kids and he turned around and went back to the house, I heard him yelling "DID YOU THREATEN MY KIDS?" And I hung up.

There was a bad storm outside and it was very foggy. I wanted to get in a car and drive it right through that house. How dare that Bitch threaten my kids! That was THEIR HOUSE! I Chose that HOUSE! I PAINTED those walls! I left those pots and pans to cook in! I really wanted to hurt her. Had I a rental car, I would have. I even picked up Val's keys and started to steal her car to get to that bitch. She talked me out of it. I called the police, they couldn't do anything about a threat they said, and they couldn't do anything about the shot. I would have to report it to Spanish Fort Police. The kids were asleep and I had Val drive me across the bridge anyway in the FOG, to report it to the police. I wish I had waked the kids up and took them. I filed a report, and planned to report it to her job soon as I got back to California.

After the repast, we went to Gennetta's Mother's home. Kennith and I sat in the car and talked. I told him I was taking Myles home with me, and I wanted KJ, too. He said he would, "Think about it." Kennith assured me that she was moving, he was separating from her, and he would guard the boys with his life. I said okay, I was just going to have the Police take me to get Myles before I got on the plane; I had already bought his plan ticket. KJ still didn't want to go with me, and at that point I was concerned with Myles seizures. Kennith promised me that she would be nowhere near my kids. He finally agreed for Myles to go with me. We would be leaving Sunday.

Myles and I arrived home. And I typed letters to the Alabama State Nursing Board filing a complaint and to The Mobile Department of Health where she worked.

About a week later, she texted me a picture of a signed and notarized letter where Kenny and KJ had signed that she had not given KJ a shot and that I had lied. They made me look like a crazed, jealous woman. I still believed she might have given Myles a shot, too. And Kennith lied. I called him in tears, and all he could tell me is that she needed her job and her license. I was sick at the sound of his voice. She was still in the home with him. He lied, and he put KJ in danger, and there was nothing I could do about it. I was so upset with myself for believing that he would keep her away from our kids. I called Jesse, and he was on

Kennith's side as usual. No one seemed to care that she threatened my kids, gave KJ a shot, and acted a complete ass around my kids. Jesse said, "She needs her job." And insinuated that I was just jealous.

I asked KJ why he lied, and he told me that his Dad and she told him that she was losing her job. He said his Dad told him to sign the note. Kennith's Dad even took her side, telling me she didn't deserve to lose her job. Jesse even told KJ to lie, KJ swore to me that she gave him a shot, and KJ asked me to just drop it. I couldn't believe how stupid these people were; did they not understand why shots are monitored? I never was told what was in the shot, what if that particular shot had been found to be contaminated, what if the FDA recalled it? We will never know. I continue to believe she gave Myles a shot, also.

I would hear that week that she and Kennith both went to jail for fighting. And when they got out of jail, she stayed in the house and put him and KJ out. Kenny and my son had to stay with his parents. Wasn't that something? The house he said I had no rights to. And here it was that she put him and my son out of it. Sounded like he was getting what he had given. She also went to the Post Office and tried to get him fired. After he lied and had our son lie to save her license and her job. It was too much for me to handle.

At the same time, she and her friend, the same one who had been spying on me on MySpace those years ago, began to harass me. They texted me telling me they had my pictures. They had the sexy pictures I had sent to Kennith. And they threatened to put them on You Tube and send them to my family. They called me stupid, and all kinds of names. I told them I was a "grown ass woman, and go ahead put them on You Tube, let's see how many hits I get. Then put yours up and let's compare." They also mocked Myles, talked about his condition, and said that he was Autistic and I "didn't have common sense to know it." I hope they can read and realize they are not qualified to diagnose my son. Myles is not Autistic. As bad as I wanted to get back at them, I let it go.

At that point, there was nothing I could do. Kennith said she stole his phone and took the memory card out. Who knows how she got them, it didn't matter. They had the pictures and I couldn't do anything about it.

All I could do was pray. I asked God to handle it. I couldn't. I gave it to God, I had to trust him and let go of the need for vengeance or I would lose my mind. I had to focus on Myles. They divorced shortly after, that was a quick "marriage" and I believe that one day she will pay for hurting my kids. The blessing is, I don't care about vengeance. Going through that helped me to become better, and to learn to forgive and release that which I cannot control. When speaking to Kenny recently about it, he said, "I have one ex-wife, and that's you." I laughed and shook my head.

Asking Forgiveness for the Sins of the Past

Over the years, the very brief and very few interactions with M had never resulted in his building a true relationship with Marcel. With Marcel living in California, I encouraged him to reach out to his Birth Father. After several months of no results with my urging, I decided to call M's Mother. One afternoon I called Ellen. It felt strange that her voice was so familiar. I apologized for all that I had done in the past. I asked her to forgive me for the part I played in all of the madness. And she did. I asked her to please reach out to Marcel and to help to bring Marcel and his Father together. I understood their reservations, the doubts that I had placed in their heads, and all of my reasons didn't matter anymore. All that mattered was I wanted my son to know where he came from.

M had served his time and was now living in Northern California. He had two daughters since Marcel, one was just a toddler. M asked Marcel if he would agree to a DNA test. When Marcel asked me what he should do, I encouraged him to comply. "It was not just M's fault. We were both young and dumb, we made bad decisions. And I planted the seed of doubt in his head, so now if he needs a Blood test, then give him one."

"Congratulations! You are the proud Father of a 5-Foot-tall, 130-pound Baby boy!" M laughed as I confirmed that he indeed was Marcel's Father. Their relationship still has not grown as I would like it to. But, at least the lies have stopped. Everyone knows the truth. Marcel has spent a little time with his family, and I only hope that they have the opportunity to bond further.

When Mistakes Come Back to Haunt You

Kennith and I had to communicate for our kids. I continued to keep him in the loop about what was going on in California. Shayna had an active High School schedule. She wanted to go to every Prom, every Homecoming, every dance. She cheered, and was on the dance team at Rancho Cucamonga High school. It was expensive. Kennith didn't help with expenses, and although I resented that. I still sent him pictures and updates on everything. Shayna began to pull even further away from her father. She would say that he showed no interest in her and her life, so she would show no interest in his. It became more and more difficult to get her to call him. And Kenny was not making any efforts to call her. I spoke to him, and his parents several times to ask them to call Shayna more often. They felt that it was her duty to call them. I tried to get them to understand that she was hurting, feeling neglected by them, and

that she needed them. It was to no avail. I tried hard to

compensate for it. I made sure that she had everything she

needed and then some. She was beautifully styled from head to

toe for every dance, and she had everything she needed for

Cheer and Dance.

Shayna Jazmine Moorer's Cheerleading Photo and Homecoming Dance pic.

That summer, I encouraged Kennith to come and visit his kids with KJ. I helped him pay for the tickets and he came and stayed in my apartment with us for a week. I allowed him to use my car, and encouraged him to spend time with the kids without me. He seemed to want me around. One night, I went out with my friends. And that's the only time I was able to be away from them. We didn't mess around; it was strictly family, two parents spending time with their kids. Kenny even went with me to a party. It was strange, and my friends and family asked questions. I was just glad we were getting along, and there were no romantic undertones.

Photos taken during Kenny's trip to California the Summer of 2010.

After Kennith went back to Alabama, he started to text me and we communicated more often on a personal basis, not just because of the kids. He began to apologize for some of the things he put me through. He began to tell me all of the things I had longed to hear for so long. I had dated, and was still dating R, and C. C has faded out of the picture, but we still spoke. We began to rebuild our relationship. I was weak. This had been the love of my life, and he was going to church now. He acted like he was sorry, and wanted his family back. He told me that he wanted to hold me so bad when he was sleeping on my couch. And that he was disappointed that I hadn't seemed open to it.

At the same time, I had financial problems and had to move out of my apartment. Shayna, Myles and I moved into my friend's home. Marisol and I had been close since I returned from Alabama the first time. Shayna was getting out of control. She was smoking weed, lying more, defiant, just scaring me with her behavior. I missed KJ so much. And it killed me to hear Myles ask for his Dad all the time.

Kennith asked me to come and visit. In October, Myles and I did. I didn't know how I would feel being in that house again. I missed my house. I had loved that house. It was where I imagined us raising our kids and growing old. It took a little while, and I felt at home. I slept on the couch the first night, and Kennith came and got me. He took me to his room, and we made love that night. Here it was, third time around. We visited, I enjoyed KJ and Myles being together, and we left. Not really knowing what would come next.

Visiting Alabama in October 2010.

When I got home, one day I was at home alone, and my cell started ringing off the hook. "Girl, get on Facebook, now." I got on Facebook and one of my FaceBook friends named, Nikki Hill, had my picture as her profile picture and she had all my sexy pictures added with me tagged so all my friends and family could see. That Bitch even had the nerve to send my kids friend requests to be sure they saw them. I had already warned Marcel and Shayna that she had them and had threatened me, so though they were embarrassed I am sure, they were not surprised.

My friends flagged them, and I sent a message to Facebook that she had stolen my pictures. They were removed a few hours later and her account was deleted. I still wonder who downloaded my pictures before FaceBook removed them. I got so much support from my friends. I was embarrassed, but I don't stay down for long. But, I couldn't let it get to me. Everything is a lesson. It showed me that when I was thinking that she was happy in my house, she was actually miserable. Everywhere she turned, she saw that she would never be me. And it ate her up. I thought I was the miserable one, but she was.

My friends researched her before I even got the chance after she did that to me, we saw her new boyfriend had a page. So, I sent him a letter letting him know what his "virtuous woman", as she called herself had done. His profile described him as a Christian. Kennith then forwarded me a sexy pic of her, a recent one taken where she lived at the time. The background would tell that the picture was a recent one. I forwarded that to her boyfriend, too. And told him she had sent it to Kennith. I don't care what came of it. I would never be as low down as her and display her picture on the Internet.

She had used a fake FaceBook profile to friend me and followed me for over two years! She was not on my mind, if she had been I would have noticed the familiarity of the name, but I didn't. She had a profile written like she was from Pomona, went to my high school, she had sent friend requests to my friends, she had fake pictures up. I kept asking myself, "Who the hell has time to do all that?" I concluded that she has to have mental problems to study me for over 2 years. I had never contacted her, did not speak to her. She answered the home phone only one time when I called, and I simply asked to speak to my kids. It dawned on me that she read my post saying all I wanted for Christmas was a photo of all my kids together, and that was shy she sent the New Year's Card.

I was looking better than ever, and feeling better than ever. She saw my friends and I having a good time. She saw me hosting food drives for the hoMarceless, Christmas Toy drives, and being a leader in my community. I had done a lot more than just think about Kennith, and I damn sure was not thinking about her enough to stalk her as she had done me. I was living, and I was content, just as he decided to make his way back into my life. I had rebuilt my life, my kids had a home, we had everything we needed and I was making it without any help from Kennith.

Single, and looking and feeling better...Self-Esteem back!
40th Birthday picture below.

When Fear Causes Confusion

November 2010, Shayna was out of control. Her grades were terrible; She was only interested in Cheerleading and Dance. She was smoking weed, and having too much involvement with boys. She had a boyfriend, and when I was visiting Alabama, the GPS on her cellphone told me she had left school and was at his house.

I was afraid for her. And I had Myles asking for his Daddy every day. I was lonesome and I longed for the safety of a husband. Kennith and I were talking more, and he was filling that same old longing I had for him. There were phone calls, and Internet video chatting all throughout the day. That love I had always had for him was back. His poems and apologies sounded so good. That was the Kennith I always knew was there. That was the Kennith I had fell in love with. That was the Kennith I had married, "For Better or Worse."

Kennith was going to church, and we were praying together and even discussing the Bible. *"This is it,"* I thought.

Everything I ever prayed for was coming into place. God was

blessing me with my family again.

Birthday Trip to Atlanta in January of 2011 with friends from Alabama.

Myles in the Special Olympics in 2011, Fairhope, Alabama.
Kenny, Myles and Jesse Moorer.

I sent Shayna to Alabama, thinking her Father could control her better. At least there were fewer opportunities in Alabama. I followed a month later. I sold my furniture, sold my Ford Explorer, took my Savings and hired a Moving Company.

In December of 2010, we were under one roof again. Shayna was attending Church with her Father. We all started going to Church at Kennith's Church. It was a COGIC church, not what we were used to. Shayna seemed happy; she was going to school and attending church. She had made friends with the other teens in the Church, and it all looked good on the outside.

During this time, Kennith's mother's health had deteriorated. Our Grandmother had been in and out of the hospital with Heart Disease. Grandma was in her 90's and it was hard on her. The family would pull together and provide care to her. Grandma was surrounded by love. As her health further deteriorated, the conversation about Hospice had to be discussed. I had gone back to work, part-time with Covenant Hospice. I had my Mother-in-law placed on the program, and some of our Aunts wondered if it was time for Grandma to be placed on the program, also.

We had a family meeting; I addressed the families concerns and answered all their questions regarding Hospice. I felt inhibited; knowing at a power struggle among the family was brewing. Part of me wanted to stay out of it to avoid this struggle, but I knew I had been put there for a reason. I prayed that God would guide me and allow me to be of service to my Grandmother. And he did. It was such a blessing to be able to provide care to her. She was such a Woman of God. She would pray and intercede for days for her family, I believe she was preparing to depart.

My Mother in law required a great amount of care. I would bathe her, provide her skin care, assist her with toileting, and dress her. I believe God put me where I was supposed to be at that time. My Mother in law has always been a negative person. And it is difficult to care for her, but I am a Caregiver. That's what I do.

Kennith began to pull away from me. I could feel it. It was a short Honeymoon period that ended after the New Year. I began to feel very lonely again. I knew I had made a mistake, but I didn't want to accept it. How could this happen? Finally, he goes to church, the Pastor is talking with me about the need for us to be remarried. Why isn't he talking to Kennith? He may have spoken with Kennith, but it didn't feel as if he had. I had come home expecting Kennith to propose, to surprise me with a ring and make us one big, happy family.

Kennith asked me if it would be okay for him to NOT buy me a Christmas present due to money issues. I had always put myself last before, I would tell him that it was okay as long as the kids had what they wanted. But, this was a new day, and I was no longer going to put myself last. I told him that was NOT okay.

Christmas Day came; I was able to get the kids everything they wanted with money I had put aside. Kennith gave me an open-heart necklace, and gave Shayna a smaller one. It was from Kay's Jewelers where I knew he had a credit account. As February came, Kennith had to go out of town for a Gig. He left his bills on the dining room table. He knew that I was always tidying up, and would move those papers. I had long given up searching for clues to Kennith's life. I was determined that this was a fresh start and that we were going to make it work.

I went to move his pile of bills and put them in his drawer, when a Kay's jewelry bill fell to the floor. I looked at it, and it showed several purchases made in December. I saw that he had purchased Shayna and my necklaces a day before Christmas. But, two weeks prior had purchases necklaces. No, it wasn't a purchase for his Mother. I had bought the gifts for his parents that year, also. I was hurt. This reinforced the fact that Kennith was still the same old Kennith.

Even when I wasn't looking, stuff would fall into my lap about K. I found a letter his friend, V, had sent him from jail. Now, over the years, V, had lived with us on and off. At one time I made Kenny put him out. V never had a job, other that security for Lyte. I knew he was not providing for his son, as my friendship with his ex-wife, Kim, had continued. And, I have never been able to respect a man who don't provide for his kids.

V would clean the house, but, I am not one to be able to go to work as a grown ass man sits in my house not providing a dime. He and Kenny would work on music, which was another crazy thing. They were grown men, still rapping about "coochie". It was disgusting. Well, as I said, over the years V had lived with us on and off. At this time, he had spent some time in jail, I think it was for some type of fraudulent use of other's peoples credit cards or something like that. I am sure Kennith was involved, and, I think V did some time to keep Kennith from being pulled into it. Anyway, so back to this letter. In this letter from jail, V started off by saying that he called Kenny three times one day, and Kenny didn't answer. Then he wrote, "I am going to call you on Sunday, and you better answer." This caused me to pause. Then in the letter V talked about how he was telling some other inmate about K, and V told K to send him a picture.

Wait...WHAT? My mind was spinning. First off, I don't know any men, or any women for that matter, who will allow a friend to tell them that they "better" be available to talk them when they call. Then, what man in jail wants another man's photo?????

And then, I start to feel real stupid, dumb, and blind when my mind reaches back and reminds me that V and Kennith called themselves "The Butt Brothers". Supposedly, it was because they like big assess. I'm was thinking then that it was because they are "asses".

I questioned him when he returned and he didn't even bother to make up an excuse. He just told me that I was crazy. No, that wouldn't be working this time. Although I felt crazy for ever thinking that he would love me right. I knew I was not crazy. I had time to grow and be without him, and I knew that I was sane. I began to withdraw. I had Grandma and my Mother in law to care for, and I continued.

Kennith and I began to argue. I stopped going to church with him. It was all just a Facade. I cannot be anything but real. I prayed, and I fasted, and I asked God to show me what to do. My money was gone. I didn't have a car. I gave up my job in California. Here I was, again. And in a worse situation than the one I left.

My friends in California sensed that I was not happy. My friend, Robin, asked me straight out what was up, and told me to never forget that I have options. I tried to pretend everything was okay. I was determined to wait for God to tell me what to do. I was open to counseling, and working on our family. But, I had realized that no matter how badly I want it, I couldn't do it alone.

Shayna and I began to talk. She shared her feeling with me, talking about why she had acted out and what she learned. She was working at Wal-Mart and her Grandfather bought her a used Mitsubishi Trooper from the Auction. Kennith brought it home and gave it to her. I asked him why he didn't have it detailed before giving it to her, because it was full of dust. It was small things like this that showed me that his priorities were still out of whack.

One Sunday at the end of May 2011, after Kennith and I had spent weeks arguing and he had the nerve to call me "Lazy." And complain that I was not contributing financially to the household. There I was, providing care to his Mother, and his

Grandmother and he called me Lazy? His sister came to town, and stayed at his parent's house and left the house in worse condition than before she got there. Even his parents, and the entire family would talk about how she was of no help to her parents, and he was calling me lazy?

I lay in the bed, praying. Kennith had gone to church and Shayna and I were at home. I rolled over and saw that he left one of his cell phones at home. I picked it up, removed the memory card and put it in my phone. Up pops pictures of a female, with video of her playing with herself and telling him how much she loved him. The dates of the pictures and videos varied, with the most recent being in May. I saw the name Ms. Reed on several of his telephone calls, and looked her up on his FaceBook. BINGO, same person. I sent her a message, to which she responded. Telling me that Kennith was just a friend, and that she would help him financially because he told her I lost my job and was only staying there to help with the kids. This made no sense; obviously she was more than a friend. She then informed me that she and another female, NJ, had been arguing about Kennith that same week. I had found pictures of a female and Kennith that he had hid in the closet. I contacted NJ. And she gave me the same info. Kennith told her that I was only there because I needed help with the kids. She was planning on moving to Alabama with her son in August, and her and Kennith were in a relationship. And yes, the gifts from Kay's Jewelry store were for MR and NJ. I was done.

I sent emails to our family, church members and friends. I was tired of everyone asking me why we weren't working out. Here was their answer. I sent a photo of him and Keta Reed. I would leave, I didn't know how, but I was leaving.

We had continued to have sex, me weak with love, and him feeling that he had that right since I was in his bed. After seeing those photos, reading those jailhouse letters, and knowing that he had gotten worse from the last time I left, I was determined to never let him touch me again.

Kennith came home mad. We argued, and we argued. I asked him to leave. Let me have time to relax, he had his family to stay with and I was on my own.

I will admit that I began talking to some of my male friends and exes during those weeks. I was lonely, and I fell back to what I had been used to in California. I didn't speak to my Girlfriends in California, or my family. I didn't need the stress. I would do something, I just didn't know what.

Kennith took the laptop he had given me for Valentine's Day. I had some of my writing stored on it, and it had all of my personal information in it. I wanted it back. We fought, and I said things to hurt him as he had hurt me. Kennith packed a bag and left. We had scuffled, and he had choked and pushed me, I couldn't believe that I was back in Alabama and worse off than I was in 2008 when I had left him for the second time. I felt so stupid, and I was angrier with myself than I was with him.

KJ and Myles were at his parent's house. It was June 8th, 2011. I was crying and lying in the bed. Shayna came running downstairs telling me that somebody was on the side of the house. It was a big house, and we turned off the lights and tried to see from upstairs what was going on. Shayna called the police. We saw that it was Kennith after a while, he had parked down the street and was walking around the house. That scared me. That was out of character for him. I felt like he was trying to terrorize me. The police came, and I told them it was Kennith and that he had taken my computer. The found him around the corner, he told them he needed his medications.

I wanted to trade the medicine for the computer, he wouldn't. I gave him the medication anyway. The police informed me that we were considered common law married at this time. That meant that what was his was mine and what was mine was his. I felt like throwing up. *"What the hell is wrong with me? I came back here for this?"*

About 10pm, the police left. I looked at Shayna and I said, *"You ready to go?"*

Kennith had already agreed to let me leave, we had been arguing for weeks. He told me that he would give Myles back to me. He didn't know we would be leaving that night, though. I wanted to call the kids, but knew that KJ would tell his Dad I was saying goodbye.

Shayna and I packed her truck. We loaded two televisions, our clothes, some pictures. We loaded whatever would fit in the car. I had $480 in the bank. We headed to my girlfriend's home in Houston at about midnight. Four hours after we left, I tried to call Kenny to tell him that the Garage door had broken again and that we were gone and I wanted to say goodbye to my boys. He didn't answer the phone.

I knew the way. We each had our cell phones and I had Triple A. I prayed we would make it all way home. The only person who knew we had left, was my friend, Karen. She was expecting us in Houston. As we were crossing into Texas from Mississippi, the road was dark and lonely. Suddenly a very large dog was on the road. He turned to the side, and looked at us. He looked like a demon. I hit him and kept on going. It damaged the car, and something was dragging on the right side of the car. I pulled over a mile or two later, and the fender was hanging. I pried it off myself. I wanted to cry, but I didn't. Shayna had to know I felt safe. We kept going. Every time I would make a right turn we would hear a loud noise. I stopped a gas station in Texas and tried to fix it. The damage had caused part of the wheel well to rub the tire when we turned to the right. I used a tire rod to bend it back some and we kept going. We pulled up to my girlfriend's home at 7am.

I was emotional, exhausted, disappointed, angry, sad, and worried. I already missed my boys and I worried that they would feel abandoned. I worried that Kennith would try to keep them from me. But, I knew that had I stayed something really bad would have happened. I was tired of going back and forth with Kenny. I didn't want to hurt him, and I didn't want to get hurt. The way we were acting and talking to each other was horrible, and it was bound to end terribly if I had stayed.

Kennith started texting me that morning. Saying I left my kids, mad because I took his mic and his mixer. I did. I wanted something. This was the 3rd time I was leaving him with everything. I hated his music and everything it stood for. It never benefitted my children. And I was tired of being the one hurt and lied to. He took everything from me, he deceived me and I wanted him to be just as mad as I was.

His sister even texted me and talked shit. They had the nerve to text Shayna, about the equipment. She texted them both back, telling them that they not once asked about her safety, or if she needed anything, but only about the equipment.

I was so overwhelmed that I called Kennith's Pastor, asking him to talk to Kennith to ask him to stop threatening and harassing me. He only told me that he wished I had come to him instead of leaving. After that one conversation, the Pastor never once to check on me. The pastor who had spoken over us, who had given me that Prophetic word that had the anointing of an Evangelist, the Pastor who had ministered to us as a family for the last six months. He didn't reach out as I had expected him to.

Karen opened her home to us. She had her neighbor check my tires. The truck we were in was horrible on gas; I had already spent almost $300. I sold one of the TVs to Karen, and I called my niece and asked her to ask my nieces and nephews for money to put into my bank so I had backup funds on my debit card.

Kennith and I continued to argue on the phone, hang up and text one another back and forth. I spent much of the day crying, and it was upsetting to Shayna. My friend, Karen, looked at me and said "Stop talking to them. Why are you talking to people that already showed you they don't give a damn? You can't reason with them, and you are safe. Just stop talking to them." And I did. I stopped answering the phone, and told Shayna to stop answering hers. His words about my sons hurt me. I didn't want my kids to feel abandoned.

But, I didn't want them visiting me in jail either. I wanted to hurt their Father. I wanted to fight him, and make him feel all the hurt he had caused my kids and me. That is why I had to leave. He was acting in a way I had never seen him act before, and I was feeling out of control. I don't know what might have happened if I had stayed. I just know that the devil was trying to push me to the edge, and it was my own fault. And so, I ran.

We stayed there until about 4 am the next morning. We got back on the road and headed for California. The air conditioning broke about four hours later. We continued on.

Shayna had a Driver's license, so she would drive for a few hours. I still couldn't really sleep. I had told my friend, R, that I was on my way home. That evening about 6 pm, he called and the first thing he asked was, "Did you check your oil?" I hadn't. I should have known to. I had been on many trips with Kennith, and I always watch and learn. I could kick myself. I pulled over at the next off-ramp with a gas station and checked the oil. It was dry. I Praised God, reminding Shayna that God always provides for me. I filled the car with oil, taking even more of the money that we had to get home. The phone calls stopped from Kennith and his family. His Mother had called asking where we were several times. They knew I was going home, but I wouldn't tell her exactly where we were. I would check in with my friend, Karen, and with my niece, Tiffany. I didn't call my Mom; she is a worrier and would have given me even more stress.

We pulled up to Tiffany's Apartments at 5am the next morning. We were home. NJ and I continued to communicate during my trip back to California. We shared information about Kennith with one another. She seemed like a nice woman who just like me got caught up in Kennith's deceit. She would go on to share with him all of our conversations, and emails. I wasn't very surprised. I would have told him how I felt myself if he had asked. I don't run from the truth. I understand Kennith's charming, and capable of making you feel like you want to be on his team only to realize he's got a full roster, and you better get used to sitting on the bench. But, I did have to cuss her out and let her know I knew she was a snake. She denied it, even after I emailed her a copy of proof that she forwarded my emails straight to Kennith. I found the emails she forwarded when I accidently gained access to Kennith's email. I swear, I am a good detective, however, I wasn't trying to find this stuff. I was accessing my own old AOL account when the family accounts popped up on my screen. I completely forgot that when email first came out I had started Kennith's account for him. Anyway, as the account opened up, I saw emails from NJ. Proof she was forwarding him all the emails between she and I.

Then, I see emails between Kennith and some people where he responded to Craig's lists ads for sex! Yuck. The links were old, so I couldn't see who he was communicating with, but the messages were there. He was asking to meet up with them for sex, and I was completely grossed out. I was so glad that I left! I realized then, I would rather sleep on a concrete floor with no pillow, than next to a man I cannot trust.

Photo taken shortly after arriving back in California. No car, No job, No man...but, not ever going to break.

The Floor, Again

By this time, I felt that sleeping on the floor was just another trial to reinforce the strength that God gave me. I had less than $200. And I tried to hold onto it. I hardly ate, not really knowing if it was from depression, or from the fact that I didn't have any money to contribute to the household.

I began to walk to get away from it all. There was so much angst and hurt built up inside me. I would walk for miles a day, sometimes praying, sometimes crying, and sometimes just walking. I started going back to church. The church was down the street, and I could walk. The Trooper that had gotten us to California was in need of attention, and I tried to drive it as little as possible. I didn't know if Kennith had removed it from the insurance, and something inside me felt like we stole it. I hated that I needed something from them.

KJ was angry with me. His head was being filled with all kinds of lies, and he couldn't understand why I had to leave. I had to put him in God's hands. There were times when I would call and Kennith would say Myles was with his parents, and then I would call his parents and they would tell me that Myles was not there. That was so cruel. I had never, ever created an obstacle to Kennith talking to any of the children. Kennith knew that he could hurt me through my kids, and that is what he did. My friends were my support, and they tried to give me the hope that one day the truth would come out and I would have all of my kids back.

I started looking for a job. My mother helped me pay an old ticket I had received, and clear my driving record. I didn't hear from any of the places I applied, including my old job for several weeks. At one point, I got down to $5.00. I kept that $5.00 in my purse for over 3 weeks, praying that God would send help.

I had an attorney working on the Car Accident Case since 2009. I called to update my address on file with them, when they informed me that they had mailed a Workman's Comp Hearing Date to my Alabama Address. It would be On July 11th, 2011. "Hmmmm, that is Kennith's Birthday." I thought to myself, his birthday and my day to get back up on my feet.

When God Sends Help

I went to the hearing, and my Attorney met with me. It was 8 am. There were two things against us. The Insurance Company had not sent Representation. She would have to call and speak to them. I was to sit tight and wait.

Okay, she spoke to the Insurance Company. They had been taken over by the Insurance Commission for wrongdoing and had arbitrators taking over closing out all of their open cases. They would be sending an Attorney. We had no idea how they would be responding, or if the case would be postponed further. I went and had lunch and waited some more.

They were calling everyone's name, but mine. My Attorney came out of the back room, and pulled me to the side. She told me that they were not arguing any points, they were not requesting me to see any additional doctors, and they agreed to settle the case.

I was awarded over $40,000 dollars! And I would be receiving a check for approximately $32,000 in a few weeks. God is good. I cried in the car, thinking that if I had been in Alabama, I would have used that money to save Kennith's home and pay off his car, and buy me another car. Only to find out that he was still a big dog. I had been spared of that pain. God was looking out for me, reminding me again that HE is my Provider and NOT a man.

Short hair...a new me.
September 2011.

Abundantly Exceedingly Great

I knelt at the altar at church. I needed to know I would have my son back. Since I had a little money I could fight him now. And I was preparing to do just that. As I prayed, God spoke to me.

"You don't have to fight. I am fighting for you. Everything that has been stolen from you will be returned."

Two days later, Kennith agreed to give Myles back to me. KJ was still angry with me, but I told him that was ok. *"I will always be your Mom, even when your disappointment me, there is nothing you can ever to do to keep me from you."* I kept texting, calling and sending him things. I opened accounts for the kids, and put $400 in his account for his school clothes. I was more than angry, when I saw a debit for a $60 bill at a restaurant. His

Dad's response was, *"KJ wanted to take me to dinner."* ON MY DIME! Who does that, who lets their son spend the money their Mother gave them for school clothes on Dinner for the other parent? That was just another example of Kennith's lack of integrity.

I bought myself a car, and I bought Shayna a used car. Shayna's Honda Civic needed work, and I put a couple thousand dollars into it. She was to watch Myles after school when I worked, and I would give her money and gas cards. I began to buy what I would need for an apartment.

I moved back into Marisol's home for a couple of months, both to save, and to help her out. I knew Shayna needed guidance, and Marisol had a daughter the same age. We thought that the girls would be better off with me home in the day, and Marisol home at night. It worked for a few months.

Shayna began to be disrespectful and unruly once again. She wrecked her car, wasting thousands of dollars. And she moved out shortly before her 18th birthday. She told me that she was grown, and I couldn't control her. And I couldn't. She would go to my girlfriend's house, then to my niece's house.

In February, I was able to get an apartment for Myles and I. We moved to a nice two-bedroom apartment in Rancho Cucamonga. I had everything I wanted for my apartment by myself. All those years of not being able to have nice things, working and sacrificing, and I had nicer things than I ever had when I had a husband. God was providing, and I was blessed. I was hired as an Admission Nurse with the company I worked for when I left. Everything was in place, for the 3rd time.

Facing My Faults

I would be back in a relationship with R at this time. I had finally allowed him to meet Myles and we would go to Las Vegas some weekends to be with R. We were getting along, but I was still damaged. And he, too, was damaged from a previous relationship. We were good together, but problems arose.

We broke up, and back into my life came C. C had been in and out of my life for years, but I was seeing him in a different light. He was talking to me, and he began to be here for me. He became a part of my life, and this put a stop to my even talking to R.

C and I tried to make it. But, me still damaged, and his control issues ended our relationship. He thought I cheated on him with R during a trip to Las Vegas, I didn't. But, I realize my not talking to him about it led to hurting him. I hate that he feels I cheated when I didn't. R, on the other hands, says he respects me because I didn't cheat with him in Vegas. I have to remember, everyone involved can view the same situation in a different way. And that reminds me that maybe Kennith didn't do all of the things I thought he did, maybe he did more.

Finally, I don't really have any more questions. It is what it is, and the only truth that matters is my kids need their Father. I forgive him. He says he forgives me. KJ told me that one day he asked his Dad if there was anything in his life he would change if he could. KJ said he never really saw his Dad tear up before, but he said, "I wouldn't have kids with your Mother." It hurt to hear this. Maybe he does regret our ever being together. I could only tell KJ that I don't regret it, His Dad and I made four beautiful children, who are my gifts from God, and I would do it all again it if meant they would be my kids. My regret is I just stayed too long. Maybe I missed the man God really had for me by chasing after Kennith.

After experiencing three breakups, I accepted that I was still grieving my marriage. No matter how much time passed, or how much went on, I still longed for this fantasy of a marriage that I imagined Kennith and I could have.

I have to realize that I was in love with the idea of our marriage and what it could be, not what it was. Kennith does not deserve me. I have to remind myself of that all the time. I have also come to realize that my peace of mind is my most valuable possession. And it's up to me to protect it.

Being single causes me to feel unsafe, unprotected, and I have to deal with that. But, there is no better protector than God. And here I am, blessed beyond imagine. I sometimes feel the anger and hurt creeping back in. And, I must remind myself of where I have been. I had a family, I owned a home, and I was a wife. I may not own a home, and I may not be a wife, but I am God's Princess, and I will not allow anyone to treat me anything less. And I have peace of mind in my small apartment, and I would not trade that for anything.

I have four beautiful kids, and two wonderful Grand Babies. They are my priority. No matter how old my kids get, they are still my babies. And though I will always encourage them to fly, I will protect my nest in case they ever need to rest here again. I made a promise to myself that before the last word is written, I will choose to forgive. Kennith and I are Grandparents now, Kali Kingston and Malachi Jayden, were both born in the beginning of 2013. I refuse to allow bitterness to continue on to our Grandchildren. I am willing to start with me. I am choosing to forgive. I have made sure that Kennith has pictures and video of the babies. I try to keep him a part of this legacy that we began together.

I can honestly say that I forgive. Everyone. And I am refreshed and new today. Every time I make a conscious effort to forgive, God gives me evidence of things not seen. He gives me a rainbow at the end of every storm.

Recently, KJ has decided to live in California with me. It caused a few weeks of tension between Kennith and I. But, as always, My God came through and Kennith agreed to let him live with me. There are a lot of reasons KJ decided to stay in California. All I know is, I feel complete having all of my babies in my reach. God is so good to me. Kennith agreed within twenty-four hours of my praying and asking God to help me to forgive Kenny's sister. I told God that I don't want hate for anyone, and she and Kennith were the two people that it has been the most difficult for me to forgive. Forgiveness has been the key to changing everything for the best in my life. As I forgave, the bitterness and the anger left.

The journey to record my life as Kennith's partner has been difficult. Some days the pain was simply too much to bear and I had to stop. Other days, the tears were therapeutic and I could feel the healing taking place. As I shuffled through our photos, letters and memories I was able to see the transformations I made. I finally feel sexy and part of me feels guilty for not putting much effort into my appearance for many years I spent with Kennith. It's strange to me how I seem to do better alone. I used to feel that Kennith had gotten the best of me, but he didn't. The things I went through and the lessons I have learned have benefitted me. The evolution of me was worth the fight. Writing this helped me to see that the best of me is not gone, it didn't waste away. I am the very best of me. And as long as God is the Architect of my life, I will not miss out on all this life has to offer.

Kenny says I have turned his kids against him. I say you can't turn anyone's kids against them. He tried it with KJ, and he failed. My kids love and respect me because of the Mother I have been to them, no matter what anyone has to say about me. And if Kenny had been a Loving and attentive Father all the time, there would be nothing I could ever tell my kids to make them dislike him. I never wanted our kids to dislike him, anyway. I have always wanted our kids to have two parents that they know love them and have their backs. I hope that one day he will listen to them, and simply understand that what he does and how he lives affects them.

Was I stupid for loving my husband the way I did? No. I loved him the way wives are supposed to love their husbands.

What I realize now is that he should never have been my husband. I should have loved myself enough to see the danger signs that were there very early in our relationship. I chose to ignore them. I had this idea in my head of who I thought Kennith Michael Moorer could be. Never really accepting who he really is. I accept responsibility for that.

Loving a man who does not know or love himself enough to be honest leads only leads to Heartbreak. And the family, friends, other women, and other children who he brings into the dysfunction are all bystanders injured by heartbreak.

God is healing my heart, I am learning to forgive, and I am so grateful of that. I pray my story help you realize that sometimes you have to let go to heal. Stop arguing, stop crying, stop fighting for attention. Some men are just not strong enough to let you go.

Sometimes, YOU have to be the strong one. You have to be the one to let go.

Finally, happy with Me! 2013.

Kali Kingston Watkins
& Malachi Jayden Gatson
with their Gammies, 2013.

PRAISE FOR INTENTIONAL MANHOOD

"Mike Stanley has lived his life as a selfless teacher, coach, mentor, father, husband, friend, and leader. His guidebook? The Bible. As you read *Intentional Manhood*, prepare to experience the biblical game plan and fundamentals that Mike has lived, taught, and now offers to you. You, your family, and your TEAM will be blessed by his work."

JIM P. TRESSEL, FORMER OHIO STATE UNIVERSITY FOOTBALL COACH, PRESIDENT OF YOUNGSTOWN STATE UNIVERSITY

"Coach Stanley writes his experience as a father of two sons, a college football coach, business owner, and husband of Sharilyn. His passion is success—not the fake kind, but the lessons that enrich his life for eternity. His most insightful words, 'Sometimes our failures teach us more than our successes,' remind us that no man gains true success by accident. It begins with your intentions—your passion to become your best self as God has designed you to be, and as He enables you to grow in His disciplines. Mike shares some super secrets within these pages."

PASTOR JIM CUSTER, TEACHING PASTOR, SENIOR PASTOR EMERITUS, GRACE POLARIS CHURCH

"Having known Mike Stanley for 20 years, I was confident I would be blessed by this book. Now that I've read it, I know you will be as well. As a man after God's own heart, Mike writes about biblical manhood as something that is worthy of our unapologetic pursuit and investment. Stories from years of coaching provide amazing insights into Christlike character development. Being a great athlete requires unrelenting devotion to excellence. Coach Stanley calls us to the same commitment in our relationship with Jesus. The lives of those around us would be significantly changed if each of us put our Manhood into Action."

TODD MARRAH, PHD
SUPERINTENDENT, TREE OF LIFE CHRISTIAN SCHOOLS

"Mike Stanley is a man's man. That's not just a statement on his toughness, leadership, or influence. This is also a recognition of his practical insight into what it means to live as a man of God the way God intended. But what you read here are not simply insights, principles, and stories. They are vivid descriptions of the ways Mike has lived for Jesus Christ for decades. You'll see his commitment to the Scriptures and his passion for inspiring men to live accordingly in our time. Prepare to be inspired and challenged by his call to 'manhood in action'—the only kind of manhood that counts."

MIKE YODER, SENIOR PASTOR AT GRACE POLARIS CHURCH

"In a day where Truth has been clouded and where strong, spiritual men are few, Coach Mike Stanley tells us what we need to hear. With years of experience with victories and losses as a husband, father, and mentor, he vulnerably shares his stories and boldly takes us to God's Word, where he found the best game plan for every man."

BRYAN CRAIG, EXECUTIVE DIRECTOR OF INFLUENCERS GLOBAL MINISTRIES

"Even as I read *Intentional Manhood*, I thought of areas where I'd become complacent and hadn't pursued change. In response, Coach Stanley gave some advice to that hard message: 'Just by reading and embracing the concepts in this book, you are beginning the process to change.'

"I love this advice. You can't change everything all at once, but you can change something by taking a small step today. If you want some sound, godly advice that will help set you up to win in life, then you'll not be disappointed with this book. Even if you're not usually much of a reader, take the coach's advice, read just a little bit, and you can still begin the process of change."

JOHN MAJORS, MISSIONARY, TEACHER ON MARRIAGE AND FAMILY,
AUTHOR OF *TRUE IDENTITY*

"In his delightful book, *Intentional Manhood*, Mike Stanley has done an excellent job of outlining key commitments to Christ and how to allow God to change a man. I love the strong coaching that comes through the book. You get the feeling that Coach Mike is right there with you as you read. Mike is talking about something that is sorely missing in our day: *authentic* Christian manhood. We need men like Mike who will raise up other men to be godly men. I love what he is doing, and I hope his tribe increases."

Pastor Gil Stieglitz, Author of *Mission Possible: Winning the Battle Over Temptation,* PTLB.com

"For all the men who were not given a clear vision of manhood, and for women who do not understand men's struggles or need for respect, you just ran out of excuses. Now that this book is in your hands, take the opportunity to read, learn, and embrace the God-ordained gift of manhood that creates confident, intentional men who will make better husbands and fathers. Women who understand this become an inspiration in their homes and communities in an atmosphere where men are encouraged to be men of CHRIST!"

Kimberly Hayes, Athletic Director, Columbus Crusaders Youth Sports

"*Intentional Manhood*—a short, simple title for a deep, profound but wonderfully applicable book. Mike Stanley lays out a powerful, Biblical presentation on how to be a Man of God. I have a shelf full of books on manhood, but few are as downright practical as Mike's book. It's obvious that he has and is living what he is teaching. In today's world, that is rare. This is not a collection of theories; *Intentional Manhood* is rich in truth and application. Any man will benefit from reading Mike's book and hearing his heart."

Bob Burney l *Talk Show Host, The Word, 104.5 FM*

"Culture is often confused about what a man is. Mike's book clears that up. He explains in detail what the Bible says. We all need men of God today."

PHIL VAN HORN, CO-AUTHOR OF *CRACKING THE MAN CODE*

"I believe we are all coaches. Mike Stanley is a coach's coach. He learned that true manhood is not bought by worldly success, but modeled in Jesus, who was so much more than just a good man. Mike is "all in" as a Christian man, a mentor, a husband, a friend and a coach. He truly tries to honor Jesus in all areas of his life. His book, Intentional Manhood: A Coaches Perspective encourages us to experience Jesus from a coach's point of view."

MARK STIER, PASTORAL CARE MINISTER, WESTERVILLE CHRISTIAN CHURCH